60 + 76

Errol Flynn
The Spy Who Never Was

Errol Flynn

The Spy Who Never Was

by Tony Thomas

A Citadel Press Book
Published by Carol Publishing Group

Copyright © 1990 by Tony Thomas

A Citadel Press Book
Published by Carol Publishing Group

Editorial Offices
600 Madison Avenue
New York, NY 10022

Sales & Distribution Offices
120 Enterprise Avenue
Secaucus, NJ 07094

In Canada: Musson Book Company
A division of General Publishing Co. Limited
Don Mills, Ontario

Manufactured in the United States of America

Library of Congress Cataloging-in-Publication Data

Thomas, Tony, 1927-
    Errol Flynn : the spy who never was / by Tony Thomas.
      p.   cm.
    "A Citadel Press book."
    Includes index.
    ISBN 0-8065-1180-X : $18.95
    1. Flynn, Errol, 1909-1959.   2. Motion picture actors and actresses—
United States—Biography.   I. Title.
    PN2287.F55T37   1990
791.43'028'092—dc20   90-38406
[B]   CIP

Carol Publishing Group books are available at special discounts for bulk purchases,
for sales promotions, fund raising, or educational purposes. Special editions can
also be created to specifications. For details contact: Special Sales Department,
Carol Publishing Group, 120 Enterprise Ave., Secaucus, NJ 07094

10   9   8   7   6   5   4   3   2   1

DEDICATION

My most heartfelt thanks are due the late Earl Conrad, the veteran writer who anonymously co-authored the celebrated Flynn autobiography, *My Wicked, Wicked Ways*. I met him first in 1967 when I started to write about Flynn, and the association turned into a valued friendship. From Earl Conrad I received many insights into the actor who Conrad himself claimed was the one man in his experience who most contained the essence of enigma in human form. He also said any understanding of Flynn would have to come from viewing him as a man tormented by the acquisition of the wrong image. The more I learned of the complexity of the celluloid hero of my boyhood, the more it seemed that Flynn was like several people jammed into the same body. It was also with Conrad that I was able to read, study and see the large amount of material Flynn had given him in order to write the autobiography. This included many letters written by Flynn and others and large numbers of photographs from his early years, a lot of which I have used in putting this book together, and for which I additionally thank Anna Alyse Conrad. Because of all the help he gave me, and for the pleasure of a fine friendship, I respectfully dedicate *Errol Flynn: The Spy Who Never Was* to the memory of Earl Conrad.

ACKNOWLEDGMENTS

This was a book for which I needed much help. I am, in particular, grateful to two gentlemen without whom the writing would have been impossible: William Donati, who shared with me much of his own research in refuting the charges made by Charles Higham in *Errol Flynn: The Untold Story*, and Lee A. Gladwin of Leesburg, Virginia, a professor of history and a specialist in research techniques and methodology. A great deal of the government documentation came to me via Donati and Gladwin. Other individuals to whom I am grateful are: Trudy McVicker, John Hammond Moore, Paul M. James, Neil Stannard, Bob Matzen, Tom Scalzo, Josef Fegerl and Rick Dodd.

At the University of Southern California, Los Angeles, I thank Anne G. Schlosser, head of the Cinema-Television Library and Archives of the Performing Arts; Ned Comstock, archivist of that vast and valuable library; and Leith Adams, archivist of the Warner Brothers Collection, School of Cinema and Television, USC. And at the Library of the Academy of Motion Picture Arts and Sciences, Los Angeles, I am once again grateful to Linda Mehr and her staff.

Contents

In his profile listing in *Contemporary Authors*, a compendium found in the reference departments of most public libraries, Charles Higham states his belief that the art of story telling should be straightforward, "Let us not be cynical, disruptive, destructive, elliptical, abstract, obscure or inverted whenever we embark on the voyage of literature."

I wholeheartedly agree.

—Tony Thomas

Any lie, frequently repeated, will gradually gain acceptance.

—Joseph Goebbels

Curiosity is my greatest addiction. This has gotten me into all my troubles, successes, failures . . . I cannot resist anything that holds out an antenna toward me, or looks alive or dead, or scarlet or putrid or beautiful. I am drawn toward light, toward darkness, toward brilliance, stupidity, monstrosity.

—Errol Flynn

Errol Flynn
The Spy Who Never Was

Chapter 1

The Assassination of a Dead Actor

By 1979, Errol Flynn had been dead for twenty years. The image was firmly fixed: cinematic swashbuckler *par excellence*, laughing cavalier and a playboy with a love life so lusty that it resulted in a cry that became part of the language—"In like Flynn!" On screen he was Captain Blood, Robin Hood, the Earl of Essex, George Armstrong Custer, Don Juan and James J. Corbett. Off-screen he seemingly caroused non-stop and died a burned-out wreck at fifty.

The image acquired another facet with the publication by Doubleday of Charles Higham's book, *Errol Flynn: The Untold Story*. Having acquired some identification with Flynn through two books and a broadcast documentary, I was interested to know if I had overlooked anything. Apparently I had. Flynn, it seemed, had been a Nazi and a traitor.

Shortly before the Higham book appeared, it was the subject of an article by Jack Slater in the *Los Angeles Times*. It explained that Higham had finished his manuscript and sent it off to the publisher, but then recalled it when he got whiff of the presence of files on Flynn in the National Archives in Washington relating to wartime espionage.

In January of 1979, Higham began to petition Washington for documentation available under the Freedom of Information Act, and by August, he had gathered, he claimed, some five thousand documents. A source at the U.S. State Department confirmed that Higham had requested and received approximately two hundred and fifty documents relating to Flynn's various passport and visa applications. At the FBI, the supervisor in charge of public affairs, Otis Cox, confirmed that documents had been released to Higham, and when asked if the documentation alleged Flynn to have been a Nazi spy, he said, "I have not interpreted the documents. He (Higham) can interpret them in whatever way he chooses."

Charles Higham chose to interpret the documents in a grand and dramatic manner. Errol Flynn, he observed, was a dedicated Nazi, he had aided the enemy in wartime and he was guilty of treason. The charge that he was also a sexual deviate seemed paltry by comparison.

I thought I knew a lot about Flynn. My first published book, *The Films of Errol Flynn* (Citadel, 1968), written with Rudy Behlmer and Clifford McCarty, contained a short biography, which I enlarged for *From a Life of Adventure: The Writings of Errol Flynn* (Lyle Stuart, 1980). I had also explored his life for a documentary I produced for the Canadian Broadcasing Corporation, *Requiem for a Cavalier*. As a schoolboy and teenager I had idolized Flynn, to the extent of collecting three thousand photos of him, which I pasted into scrapbooks. By the end of the 1940s this juvenile passion was spent and the scrapbooks went into storage. Years later, they became valuable research references. They made it easy for me to refute Higham's claim that in wartime Flynn never entertained the troops, that he never went on any war bond tours, that he never appeared in the Hollywood Canteen, and that he was only once photographed with his longtime boss, Jack L. Warner. I had half a dozen pictures of the two together.

I became acquainted with Flynn in the last four years of his life, which gave me a scope to study an old, tired, flawed hero with the eyes of a broadcast journalist intent on a story. I had watched him work in England and had seen him relax in Jamaica, and it was through Flynn that I came to love that beautiful island. In February 1958, I spent three days with him in Detroit, recording interviews for a CBC radio series, as he agonized his way through a stage play, Huntington Hartford's *The Master of Thornfield*, adapted from *Jane Eyre*. By now, Flynn was incapable of memorizing a script. I had ample opportunity to study Flynn with all his warts, and he was now a mass of warts.

Now past the age of sixty, I can look back on forty years as a broadcaster and writer. In my time with the Canadian Broadcasting Corporation, working out of Toronto, I traveled the world and interviewed many people in many places. For the past twenty years, my specialty has been Hollywood and its history. I have learned to be cautious about first impressions, about jumping to conclusions and accepting people and things at face value, especially in Hollywood. One of the most valuable lessons I have ever learned came from Alistair Cooke at a time I was preparing a documentary on him. He said, "Be careful. It's possible to be an absolute authority on something and still make the simplest mistake." Could I have been wrong about Flynn? With a man that mercurial and convoluted it was indeed possible. But a Nazi? It seemed illogical.

How could this free-wheeling Tasmanian, this man who had bridled against authority all his life, be attracted to the rigid conformity of Nazism? What would a man who had mischieviously circumnavigated regulations and laws stand to gain from a Nazi victory? Flynn's playboy philosophy, his hedonism were about as far removed from the humorless demarcations of Hitlerian socialism as could be imagined. He was, after all, an Aussie. Of all the people I have met in the world, it seems to me that the Australians, with their cheerfully disdainful attitude toward work and their lusty bent for sport and fun would be the last group Hitler would be able to entice into his constipated concept of Utopia.

I read Higham's Flynn book with the avidity of an old mathematician expecting to discover new areas of calculus. In a sense I did. The book was riveting, and its author was not a man to dismiss lightly.

Charles Higham is a well educated Englishman, born in 1931 to a substantial family. His titled father was an advertising executive and a Member of Parliament. A clearly gifted writer, Higham was first published as a poet at the age of twenty and his poetry has won awards. He emigrated to Australia in 1954 and fifteen years later took up residence in Los Angeles. Higham has worked as a literary and film crictic in London and Sydney, and for some years in Los Angeles he was a correspondent for *The New York Times* and other outlets. By the time he came to write his Flynn book, he had already been successful with volumes about Orson Wells, Cecil B. DeMille, Katharine Hepburn, Charles Laughton and Marlene Dietrich. But it was the controversy created by his Flynn book that gave Higham access to the wider realm of public attention. The controversy, the outcry, the protests caused by the book seemed to puzzle Higham. He told Richard Phillips of the *Chicago Tribune* that he was surprised at the reaction because "Flynn's reputation was dirt, anyway."

Anyone unfamiliar with Errol Flynn would have to conclude from *The Untold Story* that the word *dirt* was barely adequate for such a ghastly human being. The portrait was withering. Aside from being a Nazi, Flynn was, according to Higham: an intrinsically evil human being, anti-human, chauvinistic, parasitical, murderous, traitorous, predatory, insolent, anarchic, a man of unstable ego, free of all moral restraint, with no guilt at all, possessed by the devil, mentally unbalanced, obsessed, wicked, in addition to being an animal, a pagan, a demon on horseback, spy, prince of liars, anti-Semite, kleptomaniac, criminal, bisexual, insecure, sadomasochistic repressed homosexual, drunkard, suspected rapist and a monster. It seems that Errol Flynn was not a very nice man. The Marquis de Sade was a piker by comparison.

Defending Flynn is not easy. Despite his great success as a movie star and the apparently wonderful offscreen existence it enabled him to lead, there was a lack of real satisfaction in his life. He was not fully at ease with life and he became something that failed to please him. Despite his cheery charm and the humor—he was quite witty at times—my own assessment of him from all I can understand is that he was less than the man he wanted to be. His personality was more impressive than his character. It would have been interesting to see a psychiatric read-out on Flynn. I think it might have shown fissures in his nature, and clues as to why he allowed himself to get into so much trouble, including being accused of Nazism long after his death. My opinion, and I offer it as nothing more than that, is that inside the dashing, rollicking Errol was a serious Flynn screaming to get out.

Flynn's fifty years can easily be divided into two distinct halves. In the first twenty-five, he was a nobody, a drifter and a dreamer who showed little signs of being successful at anything. But the enormous luck of being chosen to play *Captain Blood* in 1934 triggered a second half of life that would make his name famous, and eventually legendary. The sudden shift from obscurity to fame and fortune also enabled him to indulge himself in the hedonism that was a strong part of his nature. In those first years of stardom, Flynn wallowed in boisterous fun. In 1938, he told a reporter, "I confess that I don't take life seriously ... the most worthwhile things in life to me are its laughs ... I have my health, I have my boat, and above all I'm young. I have no future nor any plans for a future. It's said that we must all pay for our good times, that there is a law of compensation which operates inevitably. If this is so, my times have all been good and I must have a lot of retribution in store for me." He did indeed.

Flynn as movie swashbuckler and offscreen roisterer is easy to identify, but what about Flynn as a Nazi spy or agent, or at the least a Nazi sympathizer? Charges like that cannot be created from whole cloth—there must be some kind of a basis for such severe allegations. There are, although set in that murkiest of foggy bottoms—wartime espionage replete with innuendoes, assumptions, dubious deductions and fragile inferences. The Higham charges contain fibers of truth but they are woven into a baffling tapestry of findings. Higham told *The New York Times* reporter Robert Lindsay, "I don't have a document that says A B C D E—Errol Flynn was a Nazi agent, but I have pieced together a mosaic that proves he is." I am not alone in finding that mosaic questionable.

But how did Errol Flynn, movie superstar, Hollywood legend, get himself into situations that would lead anyone to believe him capable of being an enemy agent, a traitor to his native Australia and to the country of which he became a citizen, the United States? What manner of man was this? Answer: a very complex man, a veritable enigma of a man.

Chapter 2

The Enigmatic Errol

One of the most trenchant observations about Errol Flynn was made by Ann Sheridan, the actress with whom he made three films. She said, "He was one of the wild characters of the world, but he also had a strange, quiet side. He camouflaged himself completely. In all the years I knew him, I never knew what really lay underneath, and I doubt if many people did."

To my mind, Flynn was something like a splendid statue that overwhelms from a distance but on close examination is found full of blemishes, yet still commands attention. Certainly he was the most beautifully heroic actor in the history of the movies—handsome, romantic and brave as only a man can be in fictional concoctions. James Thurber's Walter Mitty never had a better personification. Most of all he was very, very lucky. His pre-film life had qualified him for nothing in particular. His great good looks and charm had enabled him to skim across the surface of life. The young Errol was an adventurer—in the literal sense of the word, a man who lived by his wits and by the skin of his teeth, and with evidence of casual morality and a bit of larceny here and there. Years later he would capitalize on it all with a twinkle-eyed reference to his "wicked, wicked ways." And he was adored by millions because of it all. He lived, or seemed to live, the life of a man who flaunted all the rules and won.

But there was a great deal more to Flynn than this. A truly satisfied, successful man does not become an alcoholic and drug addict by the age of forty and burn himself out at fifty. Behind the Flynn bravura, which he never in public let down, was a lot of dry rot. He allowed himself to become a kind of amusing phallic figure and he laughed about it, along with everyone else. But it is highly probable that it resulted in a sense of self-disgust that contributed to his decline. Flynn was a more sensitive and insecure man than his dashing image led people to believe.

Sometime in his later years he remarked to a group of friends, "I think I'm going to have to give up something I've always had a passion for." They laughed because they naturally assumed he was talking about women. He then explained that what he was referring to was writing, which had become too difficult for him. But Flynn, keenly aware of his image, saw the joke and laughed—and kept on drinking.

He was never given much credit as an actor, yet, as every actor knows, to be convincing as a swashbuckler requires quite some talent. Few critics paid him compliments until 1957 when he appeared in *The Sun Also Rises*. They said he was good as Mike Campbell, the bankrupt, charming, gentleman-drifter. He was indeed good, but what he was actually playing was himself.

One scene in *The Sun Also Rises* is particularly touching and revealing. It takes place in a hotel room in Pamplona after several days of riotous fun have come to an end. Jake Barnes (Tyrone Power) comes to see Campbell and finds him sitting on the edge of his bed with a bottle and a glass in his hands. Barnes asks him how he feels and Campbell replies with a flourish, "Never better." They talk; Barnes declines a drink and leaves after a while. As he goes through the door, Campbell raises his glass and says, "Bung ho, old boy." Barnes looks back with concern and quietly replies, "Bung ho." The camera then moves closer to Campbell as the smile leaves his handsome but puffy, bleary face and he puts his head in his hands. What we see is a lonely, spiritually desolate man. *That* was Errol Flynn, age forty-eight and two years from the end of his life. Those who knew him at that time, and cared, could only ask themselves how a man who seemed to have it all—beauty, physique, intelligence, wit and ability—allowed it to slip away so soon.

Despite his Irish name and a generous amount of blarney in his makeup, Flynn was a Tasmanian, born of Australian parents in Hobart on June 20th, 1909. His mother, Marelle Young, came of a seafaring family and claimed as one of their antecedents, Midshipman Young of *HMS Bounty* fame. They had in their possession the sword owned by Fletcher Christian, which doubtless fired the imagination of young Errol, who, according to his mother, was a lively lad and loved to dress up and play people like Robinson Crusoe. His father, Professor Theodore Thomson Flynn, had just been appointed to the faculty of the University of Tasmania and would, within a few years, become a greatly distinguished marine biologist. He would also be given the post of Director of Fisheries for Tasmania and when seen around the harbor and waterways of Hobart, he often had his young son in tow. The ocean would become the great love of Flynn's life and he frequently said that it was only when on the water or in the water that he felt truly at ease with the world.

In view of his father's career, it was not unusual that Flynn would acquire a fine knowledge of the sea. But he also inherited his mother's love for the water, although he seldom gave her credit for it. She was a champion swimmer and had the boy in the sea while still an infant. Marelle was an attractive, spirited lady and Flynn obviously took after her side of the family; they were a fun-loving enterprising lot and quite different from the reserved, academic mien of Professor Flynn. Be that as it may, Errol claimed that his rapport was with his respected father and not with his mother. In later years, he would seldom have a good word to say about her, claiming that she was extremely severe with him and she in turn would tell reporters that her famous son was a "nasty little boy." Their lack of rapport doubtless had some bearing upon Flynn's peculiar attitude toward women, which was that of a man who cannot stay away from them—or with them.

Flynn was clearly not the product of a happy home. Both parents objected to living in Hobart, which they considered dull and provincial, compared to Sydney, where they both spent much of their lives. The professor was away from home a great deal of the time, mostly on research forays or for periods as a lecturer at other Australian colleges, leaving his wife and son to their battles. Flynn's sexual curiosity manifested itself at an early age, perhaps even at seven, when he swapped views of genitals with a girl of the same age. When found out, he was thrashed by his mother, who, according to Errol, referred to him as a "little pig" for a long time thereafter. For all that, it did little to abate the boy's increasing curiosity about girls. Errol was healthy, large for his age, very good looking and well aware of it, and quite rebellious. The contempt for authority and established order, which would endear him to multitudes some years later, would appear to be almost congenital.

Although intelligent, he was not a good scholar. He rather arrogantly considered academic studies as boring and chose instead to have as good a time at school as he could, which included excelling in sports and athletics. With his looks, his physique and his charming manner, everything came fairly easily to young Flynn. This resulted in a major flaw in his character—laziness—and that flaw would dog him all his life. It would prevent him from truly excelling in even the things that were important to him, even writing. As an actor, he rarely worked hard at a role; his immediate and long popularity made it easy for him to give pleasingly glib performances. It was an attitude that began in his school years.

Flynn was put into good schools in Hobart and when his father was posted to do research and lecturing in London in 1923, he was enrolled in a boarding school for a period of a year or so. He apparently saw little of his parents during that time and in his autobiography he wrote with some loathing of that period of his life, claiming that it was a dismal, Dickensian experience. However, when he returned to Hobart in the summer of 1924 to start high school, he did so with the wardrobe of an English school boy, complete with Eton collar, and a smug manner. Now fifteen and six feet tall, he was capable of besting any boy who dared to be offensive, and he was also prone to dating older girls. His school work would continue to be uninspired but his prowess as an athlete would advance rapidly.

By October of 1925, young Flynn was a Tasmanian tennis star, with accounts of his skill written up in the papers, but by the end of that year he was ousted from school. Even his credits on the tennis courts could not save him from his pranks. Among them: dropping ice cream on the heads of teachers and smearing syrup on the steering wheel of a teacher's car.

Early in 1926, Flynn was enrolled in a renowned Australian school, The Sydney Church of England Grammar School, well known Down Under as "Shore." His father's standing in academe was surely the only reason for the acceptance. The pattern remained the same—excellence in sports, with a marked skill in boxing, and almost no interest in formal subjects, although he did reveal some ability in English composition and essay writing. However, by August of that year, Shore, too, decided it could do without the presence of handsome, ingratiating, young Errol Flynn. He had seduced the daughter of the school's laundress. And there was also talk of his having lifted a little money from the guest of a fellow student. It would not be the last time such a charge was made against him.

In later years, Flynn would claim that he was virtually abandoned by his parents when ensconced in these private schools. Possibly he felt they didn't send him enough pocket money, which in view of his love of fun, might be true. But he seldom admitted that he had a raft of relatives in Sydney, including doting grandparents, who were generous toward him. It was unfortunately typical of Flynn all through his life that he seemed unwilling to acknowledge help and assistance given him. Some of his warmest benefactors, for example, fail to get any mention in his autobiography.

Flynn's expulsion from Shore took place a couple of months after his seventeenth birthday. And that was the end of his schooling. After the death of his famous son, Professor Flynn would admit that there was never any likelihood of Errol following in his academic footsteps and that school for him was simply a place to let off steam and have as much fun as possible. But in the latter part of 1926, the young blade was forced to face reality for the first time. He qualified for no profession and he had no money. His father was in England and his mother in Paris; the parents had had periods of separation and this was one of them. Flynn clearly had not been the product of a happy, well-balanced home. He had no brothers but one sister, Rosemary, ten years his junior, of whom he had seen little, all of which contributed to the "loner-drifter-dreamer" nature of Errol Flynn. On the other hand, he had a slew of assets in his favor. He was the product of a fairly good family and had the earmarks of a gentleman; he spoke with a fairly cultured accent and his charm and humor made it easy for him to make friends. He moved in the social strata of Sydney, even though he really couldn't afford to. Through the influence of friends, he was able to get a position as a clerk with the shipping and merchandising firm of Dalgety and Company.

Flynn was with Dalgety for a little more than a year. He enjoyed life with his society friends and made an impression with his athletic prowess, particularly as a boxer. He enter the New South Wales state amateur boxing competition and did well for himself. His style and skill were well covered in the Sydney newspapers. But there was something amiss in his lifestyle at this point—he simply couldn't earn enough money to keep up with his chums. Flynn resorted to a little, light crime—lifting funds from the petty cash account, but he was caught and fired. Since Dalgety and Company were not about to provide him with a reference, he found it difficult to get another job, and after a few weeks hit upon the idea of heading for New Guinea, where tales of gold strikes were luring many young men from all parts of Australasia. Presumably one of his relatives provided him with money for the boat trip.

Errol Flynn arrived in Rabaul on October 1, 1927. Ideas of proceeding to the gold fields soon fell by the wayside; the fields were extremely hard to reach through the wild terrain, the native tribesmen were dangerous, it required money and equipment, and, most dampening of all, tales of success proved to be greatly exaggerated. Flynn heard of an opening in the government service and applied. He was accepted as a cadet, to be trained as a patrol officer, with the provision that he could supply character references from his school and from his last employer. He informed the authorities that he would have to send for such papers and they took him at his word, but when no such papers appeared, he was relieved of his post. His period as a cadet lasted less than two months, and in the following two years, he would get by with a variety of jobs, mostly as a clerk or laborer around Rabaul and as an overseer on copra plantations. He also spent time as a sailor on schooners in New Guinea waters, doing some pearl fishing and recruiting native labor. He would do a fair amount of recruiting over his New Guinea years, an activity that was within a stone's throw of slave trading and about one step short of the law. Flynn, of course, enjoyed anything that thumbed its nose at authority. He also enjoyed shocking people years later with tales of his days as a "blackbirder" or "slaver," as a man who rounded up natives at five pounds sterling per head for work in the gold fields and plantations.

After two years of adventuring in New Guinea, and contracting the malaria that would dog him all his life, Flynn returned to Sydney. He had had a good time, but at the age of twenty, he was still no nearer to any kind of trade. He resumed his social whirl but work was very hard to come by. His parents were back in town, and while they were happy to see him again, they were far from pleased with his footloose, profligate ways. What was to become of their handsome, charming son? Errol still showed no signs of career interest. Indeed the only strong interest he developed at this time was a yearning for a fifty-year-old yacht named the *Sirocco*. The vessel had a colorful history in racing and she had long been a familiar sight in Sydney harbor as a pleasure cruiser. Flynn acquired the *Sirocco*, but not in the manner he described in his autobiography, which claims he bought it with funds accrued from his gold mining claims in New Guinea. In fact, it was his mother who bought it for him, presumably to give her boy some means of making a living. Rather than use it for the purpose of making money, Flynn decided to take off on a great adventure. With three friends—the Sydney socialite, Rex Long-Innes, and two Englishmen, H. F. Trelawney Adams and Charlie Burt—he set out to sail the *Sirocco* up the Great Barrier Reef to New Guinea. This is the trip he wrote about in *Beam Ends*. It was a far from wise venture to be undertaken by four underqualified sailors in an ancient ship but such is the stuff of adventure—and the stuff that makes for a book.

The cruise of the *Sirocco* took the better part of half a year—a very leisurely, haphazard cruise at that—and not long after arriving in Port Moresby, Flynn decided to return to Sydney. By the end of January 1931, he announced his engagement to a girl he had known for several years, Naomi Dibbs, and it seemed as if the rover was about to settle down. But his errant ways got the better of him, and by April, he was off again to New Guinea, this time enticed by news of the fortunes to be made in the growing of tobacco. With a little money of his own and a lot of money from associates in the area of Port Moresby, Flynn took over a plantation a few miles away, up in the hills and near Rouna Falls on the Laloki River. Flynn managed the affair well enough and took time off to join his pal Trelawney Adams, who was running a trading schooner up and down the coast. For about a year and a half, Flynn's life was somewhat more substantial and orderly than his previous two-year fling in the islands. He claims to have done a great deal of reading, and it is at Laloki that he began putting pen to paper. His success at having material accepted by *The Sydney Bulletin* no doubt gave him a moral boost.

The life of plantation manager eventually palled for Flynn, particularly as it turned out to be far less profitable than he had imagined, and by the end of August 1932, he could be seen once again carousing with his friends on the beaches of Sydney. Whatever frame of mind he may have been in—perhaps getting a little weary of being footloose—fate was about to step in and make the enormous change in his life that would lead to fame and fortune. He was spotted by John Warrick, a film actor who was also the casting director for Cinesound Studios in Syndey. Producer Charles Chauvel was looking for someone to play Fletcher Christian in his production of *In the Wake of the Bounty* and Warrick thought Flynn might fill the bill. He did indeed. Flynn would later elaborate on his discovery, claiming that Chauvel had seen photos of him in the papers due to his being shipwrecked off New Guinea, but it was simply a matter of Warrick noticing Flynn on Bondi Beach and thinking that this striking young man would be right for the part. Flynn would also claim that Chauvel took him to Tahiti to film on location, but the fact is that Flynn's three weeks of employment, at a wage of just a few pounds, took place in a modest Sydney studio. By the time the film was shown, Flynn would be long gone from Australia, and about the only immediate good his debut as a film actor did him was to improve his social life.

No other offers of movie employment came his way and once again Flynn was wondering about the means of livelihood. The prospects must have seemed bleak and depressing to him at the time because it provoked him into theft. In *My Wicked, Wicked*

Ways, he admitted to stealing jewels from a lady he identified as Madge Evans, a married lady with whom he had a fleeting affair. He rationalized that since she was wealthy, and since he intended to simply "borrow" them until he got on his feet, he would swallow his self-respect and play the gentleman thief, à la Raffles. In his autobiography, he claimed that the jewels were later lost and that he was never able to locate the lady again. Both claims are dubious. However, his theft was immediately detected and the police tried to locate him. He was searched as he settled in the cabin of a ship about to head north from Sydney, but nothing was found. He sailed to Brisbane and from there made his way up the coast, doing odd jobs, to Townsville, where he sailed—once again—to Port Moresby.

Flynn arrived in New Guinea at the end of December 1932, and in the next two months, managed to sell whatever interest he had in the island—mostly his partial ownership of the Laloki plantation—and took up the one line at which he knew he could make some immediate money—recruiting native labor. He would write about these adventures in his notebook, which he would lose, and it proves his involvement. Years later, he would recall these days to friends in Hollywood; almost everyone thought he was lying, albeit beautifully.

By the end of February 1933, Flynn had gathered sufficient funds to take his leave of the islands—for the last time. He made his way to England, via a number of ports and in one of them, Colombo, he wrote his father a letter saying, "I think I am going to try to make a career of acting when I arrive in London. I feel that is what I want to do and where I may make my fortune." Professor and Mrs. Flynn were now living in Belfast, Northern Ireland, where the professor had accepted a post at the university in 1931, which he would hold until his retirement in 1948.

Errol Flynn went about becoming an actor in much the same manner he had tackled other enterprises—with a bold front and the air of a man who knows his stuff. He invented a list of credits for himself, the only genuine item of which was *In the Wake of the*

Bounty, which, fortunately for him, had not shown up on British screens. Thus the "Aussie movie star" was able to get himself a job with the Northampton Repertory Company, whose staff and actors may have been surprised at his lack of histrionic skill, but were more than impressed with his personality and his ability on the sports field. He stayed with the company for a year and a half and it is to Flynn's credit that he applied himself to learning something about the craft of acting. But he clearly knew that his future as an actor was not on the stage but in films, where his looks and personality would make it much easier to get ahead. By sheer persistence, he got an interview with Irving Asher, the manager of Warner Brothers' Teddington studio, who took a chance on Flynn and gave him the lead in a low-budget mystery called *Murder at Monte Carlo*. It was during the production of this "quota-quickie" picture that Asher recommended that Flynn be sent to the main studios in Burbank, California.

Flynn turned up in Burbank in January of 1935 and did little for half a year except play a couple of small roles and court, and marry, French movie star Lili Damita, whom he had met on the boat coming from Europe. Damita was working for Warners and she was doubtlessly a big factor in promoting her handsome, young husband at the studio. He was then twenty-five, eight years younger than she, and they would be married for a stormy, squabbling seven years. He would speak bitterly about her in later years, mostly because of the severe alimony she clamped on him, but he would never allow that she had been helpful to his early career. However, Damita was successful in having some of the less flattering comments excised from the first edition of *My Wicked, Wicked Ways*. During their marriage, she was cautious with reporters about commenting on her husband, although it was common knowledge in Hollywood that she was tempestuous and sometimes violent, and that the Flynns were battlers. But she would occasionally admit that he was not a very demonstrative man and that, amusing and charming as he was, there was a perverse streak in him. In a magazine article, Damita said, "He loves to annoy people in childish ways. He knows their weak points and plays on them. He is a liar, too. You never know when he is telling the truth. He lies for the fun of it." They were not comments that endeared Lili to his fans, but in the light of latter knowledge about Flynn, she was speaking what is quite possibly the truth.

Errol Flynn's erratic patchwork of a life took a dramatic turn in the summer of 1935 when Warners took a huge gamble and cast him as the lead in *Captain Blood*. His overnight success in that swashbuckling classic is part of Hollywood legend. Few actors have ever rocketed to stardom so swiftly and made such a deep and lasting impression, or revealed such a natural talent for publicity. The publicists at Warners found themselves with the peculiar problem of having to play down the background (and foreground) of an actor, instead of having to invent one. Most of the publicists thought he was lying when he related his days in New Guinea and Australia. Flynn lied, or went along with *their* lie, that he was an Irishman; presumably he was easier to market in America as Irish rather than Aussie. With his name, and with his parents living in Belfast, it was a facile lie to support. The publicists did their best to cover his indiscretions (drinking, brawling and living in excess) but barely knew what to do with the letters that arrived from people Down Under and in the islands which informed them that their star owed them a lot of money. To his parents he was a rather painful pride, especially to his father, whose achievements in biology made him one of the foremost men in his field. After Errol died, the professor admitted that his son was an enigma. He would smile a little wistfully and say, "There was all sorts of publicity, a lot of it bad. But Errol didn't mind. He thought all publicity was good. Sometimes we protested it, but it was no good. He would laugh it off."

Flynn's first seven years in Hollywood were his best. Most of his films were expensive features which brought Warners a solid return on their investment, particularly if they presented Flynn as a dashing, costumed hero. At this he was nonpareil. His Robin Hood, for example, is so persuasive that perhaps that is who he might have been in a former life. Flynn was, whether or not he realized it, a personification of Byronic romanticism.

Things came easily to Flynn in his early years in Hollywood, including trouble and controversy. He was forever bothered by men who wanted to find out if he was as tough as he appeared on the screen—they usually found out he could handle himself well enough—and by women anxious to discover whether he was really sexy and amorous. Just how great a lover he was is open to question; he garnered a reputation as a ladies' man but evidence suggests he allowed the impression to build to foster publicity, and that he was in fact not a seeker of female company except for sexual gratification.

Despite his bravura facade, Flynn was easily embarrassed by personal questions and always warded them off with quips. But it became increasingly hard to do as the second World War wore on. His movie heroism caused him some discomfort when critics wondered why such an apparently fit and brave man was not in uniform, as were many of his fellow actors. He had, in fact, offered his services to the government but had been turned down. He was medically fourth rate, which in itself was an embarrassment. Neither he nor his studio wanted the public to learn that he had developed a heart condition, that he had recurrent malaria, that he had had tuberculosis and that back in New Guinea he had suffered from gonorrhea. Evan at the peak of his fame, Flynn sometimes collapsed on the set from overexertion. And this was a man who performed beautifully on the tennis courts and in the water—a total contradiction.

David Niven, who was one of Flynn's earlier Hollywood friends and fellow-carousers, left to join the British Army in 1939 and did not return until six years later, following a solid military effort. He would sometimes see Flynn in the years that followed but they could never fully resume their friendship. "I think Errol suffered because he didn't go off to war with the rest of us. It bothered him but he didn't show it, in fact he rarely betrayed his seriousness, he hardly ever unburdened himself. It would have been better for him if he could have, instead of living behind a facade. Errol was a many-sided creature."

If Flynn inwardly worried about his lack of war effort, it was hardly apparent to his fans, who were not bothered by the disparity between his screen heroism and the real world. Perhaps it was because his image was that of a man of former times. The press, particularly the British press, would razz him about winning the war all by himself, but he actually appeared in only five films which had anything to do with the war. Ironically, the best of them, *Objective, Burma*, caused him the most embarrassment. He was excoriated in England for appearing as an American soldier in a film about the largely-British war campaign in Burma. It was one of his most restrained and convincing performances but one that few people in England saw because the picture was taken out of circulation after only two weeks of British play. But the damage had been done and he endured Burma jokes from then on.

But a lot more damage, inner damage, had been done Flynn before the Burma picture. In November 1942, he was summarily yanked out of his playboy dream world by a court order. Flynn was arrested and brought to trial on two charges of statutory rape. He was acquitted, but his image was irrevocably changed and tarnished. The highly publicized trial, front page news for months, was considered a kind of wartime *divertissement*. At the end of the trial, the judge said to the jury, "I have enjoyed the case, and I think you have." Flynn obviously didn't enjoy it and he paled visibly during the five-week ordeal. Had he been found guilty he would have faced imprisonment—not that he intended to subject himself to that indignity. He later admitted he had arranged with a private aviator to skip the country in case of conviction. His acquittal was greeted with cheers. He emerged from the courtroom beaming like a schoolboy. As for his self-respect . . . he claimed that there were times when he sat alone in his bedroom with a loaded gun in his hands. But it seemed to his friends and fans that the trial had made little difference to the breezy Errol; it would take some time before they noticed that his drinking had increased and that he was dabbling with narcotics.

Flynn lived for sixteen years after the rape trial. As time went by, he would look back and realize what a turning point it had been in his life. By 1942, most of his finest films were behind him—those that followed were of varying merit, few of them really good. The flaws in his nature had started to catch up with him. Lack of discipline was the fatal fissure; he had rebelled against his mother, his teachers, his employers, his wives and even himself. The hedonistic Flynn gradually smothered the cerebral Flynn. He resented the reporters and the comedians who fed off his image, yet he did little to change their impression of him as a superficial celebrity dedicated to fun, sport, girls and drink. Yet, according to his second wife, Nora Eddington, whom he married after the rape trial, he was embarrassed by attention. "He was rather shy and he didn't know how to accept a compliment. He was worried by autograph seekers; he would get red in the face and stammer." It was during this marriage that it became apparent that Flynn had become addicted to narcotics. Eddington remembered, "He said he had no intention of becoming an addict. I believe that. It's just that he was a born adventurer, he had to try everything; every challenge had to be tackled. He enjoyed the sensations he got from drugs but I don't think there was any doubt in his mind that he could stop any time he wanted. But he didn't—he went on and on—and I think that's what killed him."

Flynn's great escape was the ocean. If he was anything, he was a sailor. One of the first things he did in Hollywood was to buy a boat, a ketch which he named the *Sirocco*, after the one he had owned in Australia. But the *Sirocco* came in for some juicy publicity because of the rape trial and he got rid of her. He looked around for something bigger and better, and settled for a 120-foot, two-masted schooner which could be sailed or power driven. He named his new prize *Zaca*, the Samoan word for peace, probably hoping he would find it with her. In 1946, he sailed her down the Mexican coast, through the Panama Canal and into the Caribbean. He and his crew became lost in a storm and drifted toward Jamaica. He put into Port Antonio, on the northeast corner of the island, without knowing where he was—and it turned out to be one of the happiest twists of his life. In Jamaica, he found an island that was an idealized version of New Guinea—friendly natives instead of savage ones, a tropical climate that was benign instead of lethal and something that reminded him of the South Seas but with no unpleasant associations. Flynn soon bought property around Port Antonio, including the whole of Navy Island, and set up a coconut plantation, a cattle ranch and a home. For a while, he also owned the Titchfield Hotel. The waters were perfect for sailing and skin diving, and he became a local character. In Jamaica he felt at home, and it was where he intended he should be buried.

But to support his life-style on his boat and in Jamaica, Flynn still needed the income of a movie star. He had long quarreled with Warner Brothers about his image, feeling they exploited him as a costumed hero, but the attempts to put him in other kinds of films, in light comedies and dramas, simply did not bring gold to the box office. His image was set. In 1949, in an effort to really recapture the old Flynn screen glory, Warners cast him in *Adventures of Don Juan*, with a large budget, sumptuous sets and costumes and plenty of swordplay. Vincent Sherman was assigned to direct the film; not having worked with the actor before, he was warned by other directors to be prepared for problems with drink, tardiness and much waiting around during production. He recalls: "At the beginning of the picture, he told me he knew I had heard about his drinking, and he wanted to assure me he wouldn't drink on this picture. He said he'd give me all the cooperation he could in making *Don Juan* a great film. I found him charming and sincere, and I think he was serious. The first ten days he was marvelous, he was never late and he knew his lines. One day, he called me into his dressing room; he had a bunch of clippings on the table. He said, 'Have you seen these?' He had just opened in New York in his previous picture (*Escape Me Never*) and the critics were very unkind to him. In essence, they said that if Flynn wasn't on a horse and shooting in a Western or a costume picture, he was pathetic as an actor. I read these things and it was embarrassing to do so in front of him. He sort of made fun of them, kidding, but inside I could see he was terribly hurt by these reviews. He was covering up. Two days later, he came on the set completely drunk, and for the rest of the time, he was drinking on the picture."

Flynn's casual approach to his work increased the budget of *Don Juan* by at least half a million dollars. It remains, however, one of his better performances, possibly because he understood the character of the part, knowing, like Don Juan himself, that the reputation of Great Lover is something of a joke and a bit of a bore. Flynn had a talent for comedy which was seldom given scope, but this Don Juan was plainly a triumph of tongue in cheek. Vincent Sherman finished the film with warm feelings for Flynn despite the problems. "It was hard not to like Errol. He was a man of great humor and charm, and he had real merits as an actor—yet he made fun of the whole business of acting. Few actors have ever been able to wear costumes and handle a sword as he did, with such style and conviction, and yet if you pointed that out to him he was insulted. He didn't really appreciate himself."

Despite their differences, Flynn and Warner Brothers set out on a third seven-year contract. With this one Flynn demanded even greater latitude. He wanted, and got, the right to make films for studios other than Warners. His first away from them was *That Forsyte Woman* for MGM. It co-starred him with Greer Garson and she remembers him with affection: "He presented out of his artistic and creative imagination, with no assistance from anybody else, a believable and most interesting portrait of Soames Forsyte, so completely different from anything else he had done that it made one realize what potential he had as an actor. It's a tragedy that he didn't live longer. There was a great deal more to Errol than people supposed; more than this rather two-dimensional figure, swashbuckling, rascally, and a great man with the ladies. I'm sure he never bothered any woman who didn't want to be bothered, because he was a gentlemanly soul and a great charmer, much more cultured and erudite than people supposed. He had a very light-hearted wit, but most of all he was a romantic."

By the time he was forty, Flynn's power at the box office was over. *Adventures of Don Juan*, which is now viewed as one of his best efforts, failed to make the impression Warners had hoped and from then on they cut back drastically and gradually moved to sever their contract with him. The critics were fairly civil about his work as Soames Forsyte but the public showed little interest. Already he was heard to make quips about death. Director Raoul Walsh, who was to be one of Flynn's pallbearers, recalls that in 1950, the actor was told by a doctor he had only a year or two left. Flynn called Walsh to his home and asked for advice. Walsh recalls, "I told him to give up drinking. He started playing tennis and swimming again. Then I went to Europe, and when I got back, I found he had been drinking heavily."

Flynn's appearance began to change when he reached his forties. There was a slight and gradual coarsening of the face and deadening of expression in the eyes due to alcohol and drugs. He was unable to perform as athletically as before. But perhaps the biggest change was mental. Flynn continued to put up a brave front but there were signs of despondency and bitterness. By his own standards, he probably considered himself a failure. His popularity had wanned and he had failed to win much attention as a writer.

Despite his inner contempt for his image as a swashbuckler, Flynn went along with it because he realized it was about all he could do to earn a living. In 1954, he decided to make a film of his own and to do it with style and class, and no interference from people with Warner Brothers. He chose *William Tell*, setting up production in Italy, and budgeted it at $860,000. Half of the funds were his and half came from Italian backers. After the company had filmed about half an hour of usable material, his backers informed him that there was no more money on hand. Flynn now found himself in the direst of financial straits. Production on *William Tell* was halted and never resumed, and various members of the cast and crew sued him for back salaries. It was also the time when the United States government chose to remind him that he owed back taxes amounting to $840,000.

This predicament was largely the fault of Flynn's business manager in Hollywood. The man had just died, but before dying he admitted to misappropriating funds, and to losing Flynn's money at gambling. To appease his creditors, Flynn began disposing of some of his properties—his house on Mulholland Drive in the Hollywood hills, his cars and some of his valuable paintings. Two things to which he clung and refused to surrender were his estate in Jamaica and his yacht. Flynn was always very cagey about money. He took the precaution of carrying gold bars on the *Zaca*, in case of extreme travail, and after his death, it was found he had more investments and bank accounts than he had admitted. But in late 1953, Flynn was hard put for cash.

The *William Tell* fiasco brought to an end one of Flynn's closest friendships. Bruce Cabot, in the years prior to his going into the Army in 1942, had been among the handful of hard-drinking, hard-playing buddies with whom Flynn most preferred to spend his leisure time. When Cabot returned after the war, he noticed a marked change in Flynn, which he thinks was partly due to his coming under the influence of John Barrymore and his coterie. Flynn admired Barrymore enormously, and Cabot claims that Flynn took on some of the mannerisms of the older actor. Some of Barrymore's illustrious friends were drug addicts and this is how, in Cabot's opinion, Flynn became hooked. Flynn, mostly for fun, had tried almost all the narcotics—opium, marijuana, cocaine and morphine. Said Cabot, "Eventually it was the heroin that got him. And even then he lived ten years longer than most who took what he took."

With the collapse of the *William Tell* project, Bruce Cabot, who had been hired to play the villain, sued Flynn for his salary, claiming he had received nothing. Flynn bitterly resented it and the two never met again. Cabot later claimed that what he sued was Flynn's company and not his former friend. He believed that Flynn's business judgment had been sorely affected by his drug addiction and that the incident was part of a much larger tragedy—the gradual decline of Flynn. "Dope is like termites. It destroyed him the way termites destroy a building, and it was a pitiful thing to see. You couldn't put your finger on it but you could see it happening. His associations changed. He didn't take the care he used to take with his appearance or his performances. Dope destroys the fiber of a man, the character, the reliability, the self-respect. With Errol it was the saddest case I've ever seen."

Flynn's home for most of the period from 1952 to 1956 was his yacht, which he sailed and moored in the Mediterranean. His drinking was heavy and continuous; had he not been a lover of swimming and sailing, his health would have been even worse. In this period, he occasionally went to England to make films and do television, and in late 1956, he was invited back to Hollywood to make a film called *Istanbul*. He had assumed his association with Hollywood was over and accepted the offer from Universal in the belief that the film would be shot on location in Turkey. Some things about Flynn may have changed but one hadn't—his love of travel. He would go anywhere in the world, expecially if it was a place he had never before seen. *Istanbul* turned out to be shot entirely on the back lot at Universal. It was a mediocre picture and Flynn knew it—but it was a turning point. It brought Flynn back into focus on his old stamping ground and resulted in a renewed interest in him. Everyone in Hollywood remarked, with regret, about the sad manner in which he had aged so rapidly, and yet, there was still something about him. A few critics even commented that his world-weary appearance gave him a credibility that he had never had before. This opinion was not lost on Darryl F. Zanuck, who decided to take a chance on Flynn as Mike Campbell in his filming of Hemingway's *The Sun Also Rises*.

Flynn himself was dubious about his ability to play the role, and Patrice Wymore, his third wife, tells of having to talk him into doing the part. It meant accepting fourth billing, behind Tyrone Power, Ava Gardner and Mel Ferrer, and it was a hard pill for him to swallow. He had never before been a supporting actor. But the result was an amusing and touching performance that won him the best notices of the film. There was some talk of him being nominated for an Oscar, which didn't materialize, and much talk of his "comeback."

However, it was clear that Flynn's career had a new lease on life. Warner Brothers called their one-time idol back to the studio, after an absence from their gates of five years, and made him an offer he couldn't resist—to play John Barrymore in their filming of Diana Barrymore's confessional best seller, *Too Much, Too Soon*. The critical consensus was that Flynn was by far the best thing about the picture. Commenting on Barrymore during production, Flynn said, "We have some things in common; we both owned boats and we made a lot of headlines. He was unlucky in his emotional life and destroyed himself. Perhaps I have had a little better luck." The comparison was deeper than that, whether Flynn realized it or not. Sadly, he seemed to tread exactly the same path as his idol, except that it took Barrymore sixty years to burn himself out and Flynn only fifty.

As his career picked up, his marriage to Patrice Wymore ran down. He made his usual flippant remarks about marriage, such as, "They marry me—I don't marry them," but on some private occasions he was heard to say that he envied people who were truly happily married. When Wymore said, "I wish I could hate him but I can't," she was speaking for a great many people whom he had treated in cavalier fashion but who found it hard not to be swayed by his charm and his humor.

While making *Too Much, Too Soon*, he met the fifteen-year-old girl who would be his companion for the remaining two years of his life. Beverly Aadland was playing a bit part in *Marjorie Morningstar* at Warners when the eagle-eyed Flynn spotted her. She had been a model and dancer for several years and looked older than her age— not that Flynn cared at this point. Beverly was a bright, lively girl and as Flynn said, "She amuses me." The two were almost inseparable from then on; he said he would marry her but it seemd doubtful. He could hardly have been unaware of his rapidly declining health, not to mention the fact that he would first have to get divorced.

Offers of work came to Flynn, but they were always for the parts of "once handsome" but now "alcoholic and decadent" fellows. He unwisely accepted an offer by his friend Huntington Hartford to appear in Hartford's stage adaptation of *Jane Eyre*. Flynn lasted a few weeks for the try-outs in Detroit and Cincinnati and then quit. He claimed the play was poor stuff, but the fact is that he was incapable at this time in his life of memorizing lines. He reduced the play to a shambles with his use of prompters calling the lines from every angle of the set. Fortunately, Darryl F. Zanuck came to his rescue and rushed him off to Africa to star in *The Roots of Heaven*. It would be his last major film. Early in 1959, he would produce a film of his own in Cuba, *Cuban Rebel Girls*, but it would be a pitiful effort, best forgotten. There would be a few television appearances but they, too, would be painful to watch. Flynn had been a sick man for many years, but he had managed to present a bouyant facade whenever called before the cameras or an audience, until that final half-year when the body began to rapidly deteriorate. The building started to collapse. In Vancouver, British Columbia, on October 14, 1959, a heart attack brought it all to an end. The autopsy revealed a multitude of contributing factors: Myocardial Infarction, Coronary Thrombosis, Coronary Atherosclerosis, Fatty Degeneration of the

Liver, Portal Cirrhosis of the Liver, and Diverticulosis of the Colon. At the Vancouver General Hospital, to which he was admitted "Dead on Arrival," the doctors remarked it as being incredible that Flynn had lived as long as he had.

His sudden death stirred up thoughts that perhaps he had deliberately ended his own life, that he had had enough of it all. He had been on morphine for years and some of his friends wondered if he might have taken, even accidentally, too much. The coroner's report is far less dramatic:

Investigation and autopsy into the death of this fifty-year-old movie actor, of Irish racial origin, disclosed that the deceased had been staying in West Vancouver with one Mr. George Caldough, as a house guest and on October 14, 1959, was leaving for the Vancouver International Airport intending to fly to California. The deceased had apparently been suffering from acute low back and leg pains and requested his host, Mr. Caldough, to obtain the services of a doctor before boarding the plane. As a result of telephone calls, an appointment was arranged at the residence of Dr. Grant Gould and this appointment was met and the report of Dr. Gould is attached hereto. Investigation by the Police Constables and Detectives of the Vancouver City Police Force disclosed no evidence of violence, or suspicion of foul play and exhaustive Toxicological Examination has disclosed no poison or foreign substance which could be directly associated in any way with his death. The fact that no Demoral was found toxicologically would appear to confirm that the dosage given by Dr. Grant A. Gould was therapeutic. The blood alcohol level of 0.25% would appear not to have been unusual for the deceased to have been able to handle without difficulty.

I am, therefore, of the opinion that this death should be classified, in view of the above noted autopsy findings, as having been due to natural causes.

GLEN MCDONALD,
Coroner.

In the movies, Errol Flynn died magnificiently. He died leading the Light Brigade at Balaclava, he nobly sacrificed himself as a Royal Flying Corps pilot in *The Dawn Patrol*, he was executed as the Earl of Essex, he splendidly depicted George Armstrong Custer making his Last Stand, he sacrificed himself again in *Uncertain Glory* for the honor of France, he took another brave Last Stand against Indians in *Rocky Mountain*, he expired as John Barrymore in *Too Much, Too Soon*, and in his last major film, *The Roots of Heaven*, he was gunned down in the African bush, serving the cause of animal conservation. But when it came time to really die, Flynn simply laid himself on a bedroom floor to ease the pain in his back and lapsed into a final sleep.

He was an incredible man, a sort of Tasmanian *Till Eulenspiegel* who had thumbed his nose at just about everything. Flynn was a mass of contradictions. In fact, it is possible to take almost any view of him and prove it with evidence—that he was a delightful man, that he was a dreadful man—that he lived marvelously, that he lived foolishly—that he was a good actor, that he wasn't—that he enjoyed his wicked ways, that he didn't and possibly felt some shame—and that, although he seemed confident, he really wasn't. His talent was undermined by laziness and his intellect seduced by sensationalism. Truly a paradoxical man; no one could ever quite understand why so many people idolized him. He once said to his novelist friend Stephen Longstreet, "The enviable life always belongs to someone else."

Perhaps the most contradictary thing about Errol Flynn is that while his life was viewed as a great success by his admirers and by his place in film history, he was also quite a bit of a failure. The word failure does not sit well with his image. The laughing cavalier, sailing the seas in his own yacht, having endless funds and limitless access to beautiful, willing women—how can that be termed failure? Difficult. But this was a man who admitted toward the end of this life that he would rather have written a few good and lasting books than to have made all his movies. Did he have sufficient talent as a writer to warrant such a sad regret or was it his actor's sense of drama seeking sympathy for something that might not have been anyway?

Chapter 3

The Frustrated Writer

Errol Flynn was not the only actor to have wished, or said he wished, to have done something with his life other than acting. Flynn's idol, John Barrymore, wanted to be an artist, and was in fact very talented with pen and brush. Whether Barrymore's own wicked, wicked ways were the result of artistic frustration or due to the flaws in his nature is open to question, as it is with Flynn. Said Errol in a pensive moment, "I don't know why I write, unless it is to prove something to myself. Before I became an actor, I nearly died of starvation trying to sell my stories. I suppose that compulsion is still part of me and always will be. Sometimes I ask myself why I bludgeon myself into spending late night hours at my desk. I've never been able to give myself a satisfactory answer. I've just got to write, that's all."

In studying Flynn as a possible espionage agent, or at least some-one fascinated by espionage, the fact that he was a frustrated writer has quite some bearing. But more about that later. First, his ability as a writer.

Flynn spent a total of four years in New Guinea and those years were the source of much of the material he would write about. All three of his books—*Beam Ends, Showdown* and *My Wicked, Wicked Ways*—contain items about his days in the area of New Guinea and it was while he lived there that he started his career as a writer. The first clue to his bent for writing comes from reading the letters he wrote to his father. I have about a dozen copies, starting in 1928, when he was nineteen. They are lengthy and descriptive, and of a kind any father would like to receive. Aside from the information, they reveal a great affection and regard for his father. The Flynn umbilical cord was clearly with Daddy and not Mommy.

What Flynn wrote about New Guinea and the South Seas proved that he had an exceptionally good eye for detail and a retentive memory. He also had a flair for coloring his tales with dramatic exaggeration; Flynn would later raise many a Hollywood eyebrow. Many people would assume it was all invention, but there were those who found out for themselves that there were shards of truth in some of the Flynn claims. Those serving in New Guinea during the Second World War would be able to confirm the tales, even discovering that some of the exploits were a little shady and that there were ex-acquaintances who did not speak too well of the famous man.

Someone who had occasion to probe Flynn's background in New Guinea is John Hammond Moore. Dr. Moore, an educator as well as an author, became intrigued with the Flynn story while serving in Australia. One bit of information led to another and Dr. Moore finally decided on a complete job of detection. The result of his investigations ended up as a book, *The Young Errol: Flynn Before Hollywood*, published in 1975 by Angus and Robertson, Sydney, Australia. In the introduction to his book Dr. Moore writes:

In August 1970, while trying to teach American history at a university in Sydney's sprawling suburbs, I attended a professional conference at Port Moresby in Papua and subsequently took a short tour of the New Guinea highlands to the north. Even before I left the Moresby area, I began to hear bits of Flynniana. The pattern was always the same—at the Rouna Falls pub near Errol's old tobacco fields, in Wau where he worked as an air cargo clerk, at Lae where he delivered labor recruited from the surrounding hill country, and so on. Flynn departed in 1933 owing much money. When he became a famous Hollywood star, his old pals wrote seeking payment, but instead each received a glossy autographed photo from the publicity boys at Warner Brothers.

In Dr. Moore's opinion, no matter how wild and improbable Flynn's yarns, there was a basis of fact in them, "Nearly all of the events described were experienced by Flynn himself or by someone he knew well. And frequently, one can pinpoint the true source without much difficulty." The files of the *Sydney Morning Herald, Hobart Mercury, Rabaul Times* and the Port Moresby *Papuan Courier* were the primary sources of his Flynn probes, plus lists of ships' passengers and interviews with those who knew him in those years.

Just when Errol Flynn began to think about writing professionally is difficult to gauge. Despite his poor track record in school, he was obviously a young man of superior intelligence and with a love of literature. The one area of school work in which he apparently did fairly well was English composition. Even his earliest letters show a flair for expressive phrasing and a feeling for words. His first period in New Guinea, 1927-29, produced nothing in the way of writing. Seemingly it was a period of adventuring; he was, after all, a lad of eighteen, nineteen, twenty. There would be another period of going back and forth between the island and his family in Sydney, but in the middle of 1931, he had his first stab at actually settling down to a job—running a tobacco plantation. This clearly left him with a lot of time on his hands and he claims that it was a time when he did much reading of great books. And possibly a little reflecting on purposes in life. However, it was his position in the tobacco business that resulted in his first major published letter. Like other Papuan tobacco growers, Flynn was hard hit by the stand the Australian government took about colonial crops being allowed into the country and competing with Australian output. He found that he could not sell his tobacco in Australia, despite Papua being a part of the Australian Commonwealth. Flynn voiced his displeasure in a letter published in the *Sydney Bulletin* on July 20, 1931:

Dear Bulletin:

Papua is one of the natural homes of the tobacco plant, and, as Papua is part of the Commonwealth and is in receipt of a yearly subsidy of $40,000 from the Federal Government, the obvious market for its tobacco is Australia. But the market is closed by a prohibitive tariff. Within the past eight months, the Papuan Government twice made representations to Canberra on behalf of a pioneering tobacco-growing concern, asking for a preference over foreign countries. It was pointed out that Papua is part of the Commonwealth, supported by the Australian taxpayer, and that a reasonable preference would perhaps mean the beginning of a large and profitable industry; also that Papua, with the bottom fallen out of two staple commodities (copra and rubber), is urgently in need of a new industry. The reply in both cases was identical—the matter was being given consideration. They have apparently been considering it ever since, for the Papuan Government has heard no more of the matter. Meanwhile, the pioneering concern has produced a splendid crop just behind Port Moresby, which is being sent to the English market, as the growers can no longer afford to await the decision of the procrastinating authorities in Canberra. It would be a near-sighted policy should the fact that the tobacco was grown by black labour prevent those responsible from assisting Papua in every way possible, when that country is being expensively supported by the Australian taxpayer. And particularly when, as in this case, the assistance would not harmfully affect Australia, which is still and must be for years a large importer of leaf.

Yours,
ERROL FLYNN

It seems unlikely that Flynn's letter to the *Bulletin* did much good for the plight of Papuan tobacco growers, but it did mark something of a turning point in Flynn's life. He had been tinkering with the idea of being a journalist and now he had the opportunity to see something of his in print. It inspired him to ask the editors of the *Bulletin* if he might be their New Guinea correspondent. He was invited to send in occasional articles describing life and customs in the islands; they printed seven of his pieces. The pay was minuscule, but in Australian literary circles, merely to have something accepted by the popular Aussie paper was considered an accomplishment.

During his last period in New Guinea, the end of 1932 and the first three months of 1933, Flynn kept a notebook. The writing does not suggest that it was intended for publication, except possibly when later revised and expanded. He lost this notebook before leaving the island and it was located in a hotel in Salamaua in 1935. For various reasons, the notebook never found its way back to him. But excerpts from it began to turn up in newspapers in Australia and the islands after his death. His autobiographical *My Wicked, Wicked Ways* provoked a lot of comment, and quite some protest, in the lands "Down Under," mostly from a few people who had been involved with him and felt that he grossly exaggerated some of his adventures—at their expense. As a consequence, a few passages were deleted from the second printing of Flynn's best seller. The lost notebook was then quoted in articles dealing with the autobiography, notably in the *Pacific Islands Monthly* in November of 1960, in which journalist Stuart Inder gave his version of the somewhat mysterious Flynn saga in the South Seas.

Flynn's New Guinea notebook is a fascinating insight into his activities. It begins at the Sattelberg Lutheran Mission, not far from Finschhafen on the northern coast of the island:

Sattelberg Mission—13th Jan., 1933.
Arrived here at 5 p.m. after leaving Finschhafen this morning at 10 a.m. Broke journey half way at Yermen to give my boys time to cook some rice. Carriers would not carry beyond Yermen so paid

them off and sent to Yehu for a new lot. Cost of carrying very high in this district—they all know what money is. Sattelberg is 3650 ft. above sea level but commands wonderful outlook over the sea—I can see Umboi Island from here—it must be 80 miles away.

Queer lot these Lutheran missionaries. For the main part they are Germans but there is a sprinkling of Australians of German parentage. Father Helbig (a lay helper, one of six people at the mission) met me and gave me this room—very comfortable and I'm dog weary and a bit footsore as is usual on the first day out.

Coloured prints of Christ are regarding me dolefully from every angle in the room. He is portrayed in a large variety of postures. Rebuking (or confusing) the Elders, who have the longest and whitest beards I've ever seen; conferring blessings, etc. Why is it that Christ is never shown smiling? He must have laughed sometimes. The prints are old though, probably done 20 or 30 years ago when gaiety of any sort was still regarded as sinful.

Sattelberg Mission is the health resort for run-down and enervated missionaries. They're sent up here for a month every year to get the benefit of the excellent climate. I spotted a pretty girl when I came in today so I'll have to shave tonight. Three days' growth is no good even for a recruiter to wear. She's the little Dutch sister, I suppose—hope she comes to the table tonight. [There were three lady helpers at the mission, all unmarried: Clara Helbig, Jutta Keysser and Marie Uke.]

These missionaries treat their women folk like dirt. I stood up last night when Karchner's wife came into the room at Kinschhafen and only succeeded in embarrassing everyone present! It was a quite unprecedented occurrence for the entrance of a woman to be more than curtly acknowledged by a sort of grunt. The idea is for all the men to sit down and eat what the women bring in at odd intervals. When in Rome do as the Dagoes do, thenceforth I kept my seat and grunted.

They sing grace in German before every meal. I very nearly laughed aloud last night at a young Bavarian, newly arrived in the country, who was making the bravest effort to lower the tone of his naturally high falsetto voice. He had fully a dozen hairs in his beard.

Long day's march tomorrow—hope to make the Hube country in

four days from here. If the rain holds off may make it in three. If it doesn't I won't be able to cross the Waria River, perhaps for a week. Thank God I brought 2 bottles of O.P. rum and the Bible, and will thus have both drink and something to read. Have often wanted to read the Bible—I believe it is very entertaining and instructive. There goes the kai-kai (dinner) bell. Hungry lot these missionaries, so I'd better get along or the board will be cleared.

14th.

Stayed at Sattelberg today and rearranged my equipment for cheaper carrying. The paramount luluai of the District Selembe came up to see me this evening. We had a long discussion, with Wasange and Tutuman, the two tultuls, being present. (A luluai was a headman or chief confirmed by the territorial administration; a tultul was a native government official and interpreter in a village.) The old man is a very distinct personality, quite a superior type. He has agreed to help me recruit after, no doubt, making extensive inquiries about me from my own boys, summing me up by the text of our talk and the added incentive of Kyle's message brought by Tutuman. He has agreed to send out three tultuls in different directions—Tutuman to go to the Waria River, Inge to go to Mape, and Sambar to the beginning of the Hube country. They will meet me at Fior Village in four days time (Saturday).

Fior, Wednesday, 15th.

Left Sattelberg after lunch at 2 p.m. and arrived at Fior at 4:30. The track is about the best I have found inland and very beautiful besides. Crossed three mountain streams, each one dammed up at the crossing into crystal clear pools. Bathed in the last one; first bath in three days. These pellucid pools were typical of New Guinea's specious beauty. They were fed by a sparkling stream flowing over bright limestone and fringed by capiac palms and coconuts. Several varieties of orchids were flowering among the surrounding undergrowth.

I sent carriers on ahead and shedding singlet and shorts leapt joyously into the cold water and lay there, lazily enjoying the rare sensation of a plunge bath and admiring my surroundings. As I lay there floating I noticed what I took to be innumerable small black twigs attaching themselves one by one to my body, but took little notice of them. Then horrible thoughts occurred to me. I jumped up hurriedly and found my fears realized. I was covered in leeches who obviously hadn't had a square meal in months.

Luckily I had matches with me so spent an hour burning them off, a proceeding which was watched with keen interest by some ten boys who had come back along the track to find me. If leeches are removed by any other method except burning their tails to make them release their hold, a tropical ulcer will almost invariably form on the spot. I now looked like a leopard, after dabbing myself with iodine on the bites.

Thursday, 16th, Fior Village.

The mission has obviously benefitted these people greatly in a number of ways. They have good roads, 20-odd head of cattle bought from the mission and bred up from an original three or four head. I know of no other natives who own a herd of cattle. They also grow English potatoes, kohlrabi, tomatoes. This morning I bought 24 green corn cobs, a dozen or so taroes for a shilling; a pineapple and half a dozen cucumbers were thrown into the bargain.

I think Wasange will get me a recruit here.

There is a little stream running right through this village and the rest house is situated a hundred yards or so from the village. Consequently I have no giant and irrepressible native pigs and dogs to annoy me. I thought at first I might get a little privacy too, but that is expecting too much. My every action has been keenly observed by at least 50 pairs of eyes ever since I arrived. But I'm very comfortable here and waiting until Saturday is not going to be so bad as I thought, particularly as corn, eggs and fruit are plentiful and of course very cheap.

Was very amused last night. My three Aitape boys, being in a strange country and having been used to finding enemies if they strayed a yard beyond their own hunting grounds in Wapi, have been scared stiff ever since they left the coast. An old woman brought them some taro last night. Although very hungry they examined it dubiously and then asked Wasange, who was sitting down outside their house, 'Are you sure this food is not poisoned?'

Wasange couldn't understand what they were asking at first and they had to repeat the question several times. When he did, he and the entire gathering burst out laughing at my bushmen. With good cause, of course, as I suppose this village has been peaceful for ten years or so. But it was not a ridiculous question. After all, only two days' march further in, in the Hube, they would not stop at a small thing like poison if they thought there was something to be gained from it.

I hear there is some trouble in Hube over a woman. Two villages are about to fight, so the talk goes. If it's right, things couldn't be better for me. Am bound to get recruits, probably from both villages if there's a fight as they'll want to get away to escape reprisals later.

17th, Fior Village.

First boy this morning—good stamp of native, too. He'll look well leading an ox about, although he doesn't suspect it yet. He thinks he's going to be my cook. This is a very good omen—to get a boy from the chief's village means that I'll almost certainly get as many as I want from other villages.

Big 'talk-talk' last night. The chief and his two tultuls came along and we discussed everything under the sun, including the late war, which appears to cause much amusement and astonishment. That all the white men should indulge in extensive fighting among themselves after having given them, the black men, the very strictest injunctions against fighting, with prompt and severe punishment for disobedience, must, I suppose, appear to them somewhat paradoxical. It must have chafed them a bit when they heard details of the Great War and were themselves prevented from carrying out those periodical raids and sorties against the neighbouring villages, which used to be their favourite occupation and hobby before we came along and told them they had to be friends.

18th, Fior.

Two more boys, making three now. Excellent going. Went down to the Bun River yesterday—very peculiar formation, mainly a sort of limestone bottom with no wash in the river bed to speak of at all. Good looking wash on both banks though with no overburden more than 2 or 3 feet at any part. Will wash a few dishes down there tomorrow although it's very unlikely if there's even colours. I believe all these rivers were well prospected years ago by the German missionaries and others.

Have just finished reading *The Good Companions*. Wonderful. Can Priestley ask for anything more from life than that gift of expression? I felt I knew personally every one of those characters at the end. Especially Micham Moreton—if he had been drawn from old Simpson, ex-actor-manager, now sandalwood king of Papua, he couldn't have been described more faithfully.

Three more boys tonight.

19th, Fior.

The rush has set in properly. Tutuman came back with 7 boys, which makes 13 and I'll have two more tomorrow.

As all my boys come from the purlieus of this district, all the old men of Fior decided to read me an address. It was rather amusing. The entire village gathered round me while I sat in the middle of the circle on a tucker box. One old grey beard then got to his feet and began to harangue me in forcible but quite incomprehensible terms as he spoke in his own language.

I however nodded solemnly at each pause and later had his speech interpreted. He said in effect that Fior had given me all their young men and I must look after them well. He enjoined me that I must not sell any of them and when their time had finished must bring them back myself, and then I would be given new boys to take their place. He then wound up by stating that although he was talking to me in strong words, I must not think he was 'cross'—and when I came would I bring him a dog? He then asked me, through the interpreter, if I would shake hands with him and I did.

20th, Fior.

Broke camp this morning having recruited 16 boys (with my 3 Aitapes makes 19) and proceeded.

Flynn's account of the recruiting expedition ends with the above notation. But the notebook continues with observations on sundry things, mostly, it would seem, as notes to be used later for use in another form. The manner of note-taking suggests the work of a journalist. Ironically, since this notebook was lost, Flynn would have to rely on his memory when he came to write about his New Guinea experiences. His memory was good. But to get back to the notebook for a moment: it ends with some introspective ramblings upon his then philosophy toward life, and they are of interest to the Flynn detective because they give some insight into his plans for attacking life. It seems obvious that the years of being footloose and aimless are beginning to tell on twenty-three-year-old Errol and that there is an appetite for something more substantial. Seemingly his first point after leaving New Guinea was meant to be China. This never came about; he proceeded to England, with stops in places like Hong Kong and Shanghai. However, these were his views in early 1933:

I am going to China because I wish to live deliberately. New Guinea offers me, it is true, satisfaction for the tastes I have acquired which only leisure can satisfy. I am leaving economic security and I am leaving it deliberately. By going off to China with a paltry few pounds and no knowledge of what life has in store for me there, I believe that I am going to front the essentials of life to see if I can learn what it has to teach and above all not to discover when I come to die, that I have not lived.

We fritter our lives away in detail, but I am not going to do this. I am going to live deeply, to acknowledge not one of the so-called social forces which hold our lives in thrall and reduce us to economic dependency. The best part of life is spent in earning money in order to enjoy a questionable liberty during the least valuable part of it. To hell with money! Pursuit of it is not going to mould my life for me. I am going to live sturdily and Spartan-like, to drive life into a corner and reduce it to its lowest terms, and if I find it sublime I shall know it by experience—and not make wistful conjectures about it conjured up by illustrated magazines. I refuse to accept the ideology of a business world which believes that man at hard labour is the noblest work of God. Leisure to use as I see fit!

One can never become a skillful reader or acquire the ability to appreciate books, unless one first cultivates a keen sense of the relative value of things; for this sense is the quintessence of true education and culture. To learn what is worth one's while is the largest part of the art of life.

Time, for example, just one hour of time is far more important than money, for time is life. Whenever you waste your time over printed words that neither enlighten or amuse you, you are, in a sense, committing suicide. The value, the intrinsic value, of our actions, emotions, thoughts, possessions, way of life, occupations, of the manner in which we are living—this is the thing to be determined; for unless we are *satisfied* that any of these things have true value, even if only relative, our lives are futile, and there is no more hopeless realization than this.

It is interesting to speculate Flynn's reaction to the above entry had he been able to read it toward the end of his life. At the age of twenty-three and just about to depart New Guinea—never to return—and proceed to England with no definite plans, he would have no idea of the fame and wealth that would shortly be his. Was he true to the above stated principles? For a large part, yes. His contempt for big business and money would prove somewhat hypocritical, since he would earn millions and display a keen appetite for high earnings and all it could buy. There would be nothing "Spartan-like" about Flynn's lifestyle as a celebrity. Whether he lived "deeply" is open to question, but he certainly lived fully and widely. He did not fritter away his life in mundane detail and he surely tackled life with great gusto and little respect for conventions. True to his manifesto, he did not acknowledge any of life's social forces "which hold our lives in thrall" and if he did not quite find "what is worth one's while" no one can fault him for not trying.

After he left New Guinea, Flynn's life as a writer went into hiatus. He did not appear in print again until early 1937, by which time he was a "name," which made getting into print much easier, especially with a yarn titled "I Have Killed!" which titillated the readers of *Screen Guide* with his telling of New Guinea exploits. That he claimed some of the exploits of others as his own was beside the point. Flynn believed that a good yarn is a good yarn.

Flynn lost no time in turning his fame as a movie star to his advantage as a would-be writer, particularly in the first two years. But writing was hard work and acting was not. The vast income and the vast opportunities it afforded for enjoying life gradually sapped his resolve to sit at a typewriter for long hours and sweat out stories. However, at the start of that celebrated career, Flynn did indeed spend some time pounding the keys. From that period came a stream of magazine articles and his first book, *Beam Ends*, possibly his best work. The title of this 1937 book refers to the nautical term for sailing a vessel with more bravado than knowledge—by its beams. It covers the half year he and three friends spent sailing the old yacht *Sirocco* from Sydney to New Guinea in 1930. It is a lively tale, jauntily written, and except for an invented ending in which the ship is wrecked, it hews fairly closely to the truth. The letters he had written to his father during the voyage probably came in handy as research material.

Beam Ends met with respectable reviews and public response, although far short of being a best seller. Critics noted that Flynn had a way with words. Be that as it may, nine years elapsed before he produced another book. This was titled *Showdown*. The book's vague title did little to draw attention. It fared less well than *Beam Ends*. By now his image as a Hollywood swashbuckler, off screen and on, worked against the idea of him as an author. How could such a hedonistic movie star be capable of writing anything worth reading? Already the image was undermining whatever hopes Flynn had of being taken as a man of artistic, intellectual substance.

Showdown is a novel but clearly autobiographical. Its main character is a young Irishman named Shamus O'Thames, whose adventures around New Guinea occurred in the same years Flynn was there. His experiences as a drifter living by his wits sound Flynnian. The plot is pedestrian and the characters rather hollow, but when the author deals directly with Shamus, the book comes alive. Shamus is of good British background, courtly of manner, even a little Chesterfieldian, he is fascinated with beautiful women and his notions of gallantry and idealism are Byronic. He is very much the individual, certainly not a part of the main stream of life, and perhaps a bit of a lost soul. In short, Shamus is Errol.

There are sections of *Showdown* that indicate quite some writing talent but they all deal with ships or nautical matters or descriptions of places. Flynn was clearly a man who felt at ease below the waves:

> The coral was alive with thousands of bright multi-colored fish who gazed up at him marbled-eyed as he glided noiselessly above them in the clear aquamarine, only enough of his face out of the water so that he could breathe. He paid no attention to them. He was looking systematically through the water, searching carefully down into every rocky cave and inlet below, peering closely into the dark caverns, in and around the kelp beds and monstrous submarine trees of tentacled seaweed. Fascinated as always by the wondrous teeming world which lies below the surface, he searched on, letting his body eddy and shift with the undulating current, watching the bright sea gardens moving and swaying in slow and graceful rhythm below.

And Flynn is particularly good whenever he describes something that is patently autobiographical:

> At Rabaul he jumped ship and, with a few pounds in his pocket, set out to satisfy his appetite for the South Seas in an attempt to swallow all of Melanesia at a sitting. Six years has passed since then.

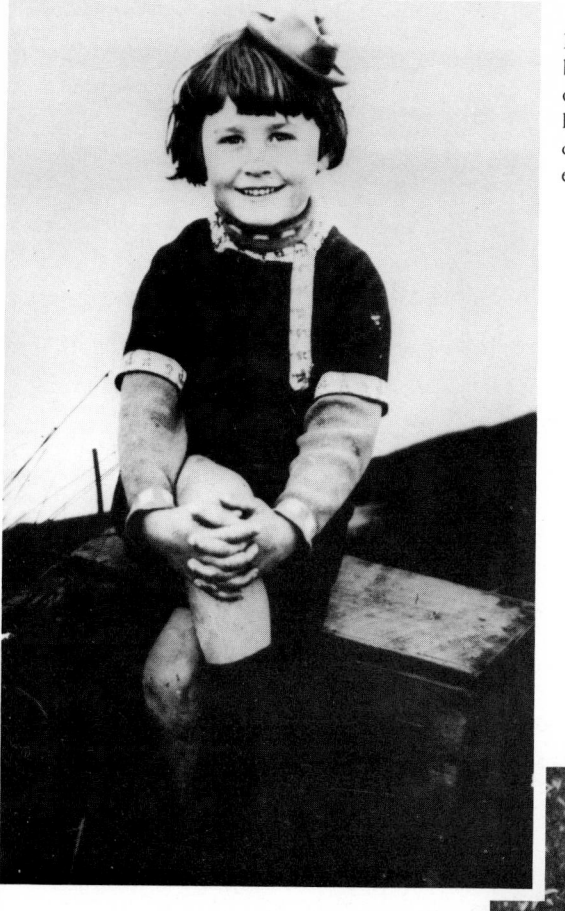

Four-year-old Errol Leslie Flynn. On the back of this photo, taken in the backyard of the family home in Hobart, Tasmania, his mother wrote, "Errol always liked to dress up." Was he playing Robin Hood even then? (Earl Conrad Collection)

Fifteen-year-old Errol with sister Rosemary, ten years his junior. (Earl Conrad Collection)

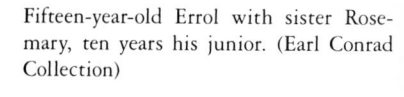

On a beach in Sydney, a gawky sixteen on the way to manhood. (Earl Conrad Collection)

Still sixteen, and pretending to be a good scholar, a role at which he was not very good. (Earl Conrad Collection)

A role at which young Errol was very good—sailor, here with his mother, taking a spin around Sydney harbor in 1926. (Earl Conrad Collection)

On board the *Sirroco* on the voyage along the Great Barrier Reef in 1930, the subject of Flynn's book *Beam Ends*. With him are Charlie Burt and Trelawney Adams. The picture was taken by the fourth member of the crew, Rex Long-Innes.

En route to New Guinea from Sydney, the first trip, 1927. (Earl Conrad Collection)

Plantation supervisor Flynn at Laloki, New Guinea, 1932. (Earl Conrad Collection)

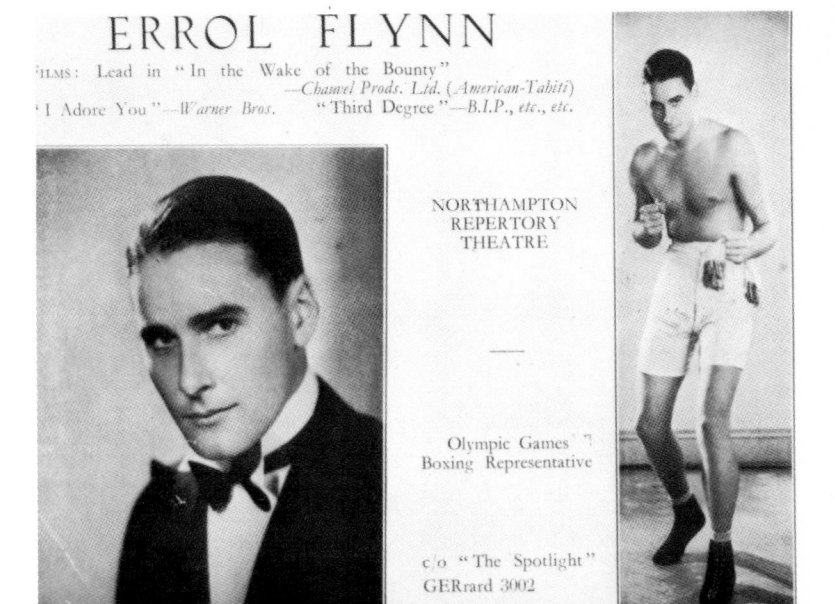

Film debut, as Fletcher Christian in *In the Wake of the Bounty*, made in Sydney in 1933.

In London in 1934, Flynn registered himself with *Spotlight*, the British theatrical directory, inventing a few credits for himself, including the claim to have been in the 1928 Olympic Games. He was at the time with the Northampton Repertory Company.

ERROL FLYNN

FILMS: Lead in " In the Wake of the Bounty "
—*Chauvel Prods. Ltd.* (*American-Tahiti*)
" I Adore You "—*Warner Bros.*   " Third Degree "—*B.I.P.*, *etc.*, *etc.*

NORTHAMPTON
REPERTORY
THEATRE

Olympic Games
Boxing Representative

c/o " The Spotlight "
GERrard 3002

Photos : Sasha.   Height 6 feet 1 inch

The Big Break: playing the lead in the British Warner Bros. picture *Murder at Monte Carlo* in late 1934. With him are Eve Gray, Molly Lamont and Paul Graetz.

Filming the duel with Basil Rathbone in *Captain Blood*, on the beach in Laguna, California. Sitting on the rock with his legs crossed is martinet director Michael Curtiz. (Paul James Collection)

The first Mrs. Errol Flynn—Lili Damita, shortly after their marriage in 1935. (Paul James Collection)

The giddy Hollywood social life of 1936. At the Ambassadors Ball, with chum David Niven, Mrs. Lewis Milestone and costar Olivia de Havilland. (Trudy McVicker Collection)

In 1936, Hermann Erben received this autographed photo from his movie star friend: "To Hermann, and joint memories of our travels together. Errol." (Trudy McVicker Collection)

He had stoked on tramp steamers from the Bismarck Archipelago to the New Hebrides. He had bought wood carvings on Iwa to sell to government recruits at Port Moresby, had joined a gold-hunting party on Woodlark, and netted ten pounds for his share of their scant find made before natives drove them off; he had handled the broad wooden clubs and carved and painted ebony shields of the Trobriands and learned there how to use the gall of a certain fish to poison arrowheads. He had solved the mysterious question of the "bush telegraph" by teaching himself to read the signals pounded on drums, which can send a message to distant natives on New Guinea almost as fast as modern telegraph. On Goodenough Island he had learned, at the cost of a month's lameness, how natives discourage those who would track them by placing tiny foot spears in their trails. Along the Gulf of Papua he had avoided losing his head to the Kuku Kuku only by lying almost motionless in a spot in the jungle for two days. He had learned from natives how to spend incredibly long minutes submerged and how to kill fish, not with a fishing line, but under water. Along the Fly River he had seen a native commit suicide by climbing to the top of a coconut tree and fling himself, head downwards, to the ground. At Wedau, he had watched nursing women fish by leaning over a stream and milking their breasts into the water, then quietly scooping up with a hand net the little fish that rose to the cloudy bait. He felt he had seen something of that which he had sought.

The failure of *Showdown* to make much impression on the literary world was a disappointment for Flynn. A man of stronger resolve might have forged on, but by 1946, the soft, easy side of his nature had already gained the upper hand.

The last article he wrote for a Hollywood magazine was titled "I Do What I Like," written for *Screen Guide* in 1950. It is perhaps the most revealing of all such pieces by him and its very title sums up the Flynn creed. He did precisely what he liked all his life, and paid the price. Now forty-one, the article shows a considerable change of attitude from his early devil-may-care days in Hollywood. There is an undercurrent of regret in this piece and some appreciation for what fame had brought him. It indicates a more introspective side of a man everyone assumed to be a total extrovert:

I DO WHAT I LIKE*

Friends have been telling me for years that I'm among the luckiest of men. It's always been hard for me to agree with them. I've had my share of troubles and everything I own today, including whatever freedom and peace of mind I possess, has been bought with an equal share of worry and work.

Of late, however, I begin to realize what they mean. Few people in life are fortunate enough to find a niche for themselves which enables them to live in approximately the way they think the most desirable. Acting, or some other form of artistic endeavor, is the only way I could have earned my living while exercising my yen for travel and adventure. Yet, this freedom has not been without its cost.

For one thing, while I appreciate any attention I may receive in public, I must admit that crowds terrify me and I hate the feeling I am on exhibit all the time. I want to be one of the crowd, to relax, be myself, instead of being followed and inspected by watchful and often critical eyes wherever I go.

When I first came to Hollywood, I enjoyed whatever fame I had but gradually it began to pall on me and from now on I want more privacy, especially in matters of my personal life. I happen to be a guy who enjoys solitude on occasion and there are times when my idea of heaven is just to be alone and I mean completely alone, with perhaps a book about ships and the sea which have always fascinated me.

The dream of retreat from the world is a common one. Almost everyone has his desert island, his Tahiti, Shangri-La, or whatever you may call it. Perhaps as much as any man, I have attempted to find this personal retreat from civilization. The closest I have ever come to attaining isolation from the world are the times when I am at sea, aboard my ship, the *Zaca*. But even then, there is the wireless and you must come to port some day.

Take my word for it, no matter where you seek to hide, the world will soon seek you out.

And, when you come to think of it, someone who professes to be an actor cannot very well withdraw from life. Even acting begins with living. If my job as an actor is to interpret life, I must draw material from primary sources. An actor, like any other artists, must lose himself in the stream of life. Only from life can he draw the knowledge of humans that will enable him to project their foibles, loves and hatreds on the screen.

I think it fortunate that Warner Brothers have allowed me to make mostly historical and outdoor dramas, like my current film. These are much more agreeable to my temperament than the suave dramatics of boudoirs and drawing rooms. Making romantic, historical dramas, I find myself in an atmosphere I love and it's easier to combat my restlessness.

It's no secret by now that a wild desire to travel is my predominant characteristic. The days of my poverty and vagabondage still come back to me now with a nostalgia that has the force of a blow. It's pleasant to remember I had few worries then and practically no financial responsibilities. I felt rich when I had accumulated $25. No one had invested millions on me. Yes, it was pleasant to be irresponsible and carefree—but these days there doesn't seem to be any geography left in which one can be irresponsible and carefree.

Naturally restless, however, I frequently find myself rebelling inwardly at the deadly routines of picture making. I get the feeling that life is slipping by me—the time is passing and I am not living fully. When this feeling of restlessness comes over me, I have to remind myself how fortunate I am to be able to earn my living as an actor.

How else could I combine work and travel so successfully. I have just completed a western for Warner Brothers entitled *Rocky Mountain,* in which my co-star is lovely Patrice Wymore. The picture was filmed on location in New Mexico. I learned intimately about a part of the United States I had never visited before. When I say intimately, I know whereof I speak—I'm still trying to scrub particles of New Mexico out of my skin.

It was an enjoyable and interesting experience, however, and by the time you read this, I will be in France, making my first independent production, *The Bargain.** This is truly an exciting project. Much of the action of the picture will be filmed aboard the *Zaca*. The rest will be made in Nice—although the picture actually is laid in 18th century New Orleans!

The reason for this seemingly-strange location is that Nice today resembles the old French crown colony of New Orleans much more than does that bustling Louisiana metropolis today.

During the past year, I have been to India to film *Kim* for MGM, made a tour of Europe and now am on my way back to Europe for my own picture. What more could someone born with the itch to travel ask from his work?

In the years to come, I intend to work as much and as hard as— perhaps even harder—than I have done in the past. Because of the new freedom I now enjoy, however, I intend to plan my work so that I can combine it with my wanderings. I want to make motion pictures in all the far, exotic places of the world.

Since I first came to Hollywood, my attitude about a number of things has changed considerably. I once looked upon all work with sheer loathing—as a matter of fact, there were those who said I was incurably lazy. Lazy? Sure. But not incurably. Today I look upon work—sincere, honest work—as man's normal function and one of the few worthwhile things he does.

I don't mean to imply that I am ambitious in the accepted sense of the word. I have no desire to excel others—to win an Academy Award, for example. I merely desire to be creative—to leave the world something I have created—whether it be a book, a motion picture, a painting or whatever—that will add to its beauty, knowledge, understanding.

Most of all, however, in the years to come, I desire to achieve freedom—to do what I like, to go where I like, with whom I like; to choose my own friends; to avoid pretense; to maintain my integrity, both as a man and an actor.

*Released in 1951 as *The Adventures of Captain Fabian*.

Errol Flynn kept notebooks, not exactly diaries but more like extended ruminations about life in general. He became more philosophical with time and his last notebooks reflect a generally wry and frequently dour impression of humankind. They are not the notes of a truly happy man and they reveal a side of him at variance with the man who amused people with quips like, "My main trouble lies in trying to balance my gross habits with my net income," and, "I allow myself to be known as a colorful fragment in a drab world." He turned over all this material to Earl Conrad when it came time to do the autobiography. The most surprising entry is one he wrote in Rome in 1953 and gave the title, "Faith."

FAITH?*

Some say that we shall never know God's purpose, that there is no God nor any purpose, that we humans are like the ants crushed under a boy's foot for the fun of it.

But then there are those who will tell you with firm conviction that never a flea jumped from a dog's back that God didn't know of.

What is Faith? And why are you born with or without it? For certainly, from what I have observed in this life, Faith is not a thing you develop. On the contrary, if I have developed anything definite it is a dull smouldering anger at the abysmal mystery of my presence on this earth, with not the least clue to any reason for it; a mystery that probably not even death will solve for me. Why am I alive?

What, then, is Faith? In what? Today, in my early forties I find myself in a state of tortured confusion where my every past action or experience, my daily movements are measured and appraised by one who does not seem to be myself; an alter ego who stands by with detached and contemptuous mien, sneering at the bumbling efforts of a human in search of a soul; a human daily more wrought upon and bewildered by the external questions: "Whence do I come? What am I? Whither do I go?"

Swept by doubt, desperately seeking just one little sign from Heaven—the sign that those of Faith do not demand, I am carried along like duckweed down a Chinese river, feeling yet always denying the existence of a benign Deity, knowing so goddamn well in my heart that I have reached the supreme goal of egoistic existence. For what?

Faith? Why does it elude me? Why cannot I find peace of mind like those I envy? Those who have listened and heard and felt, and having done so, contritely let fall all other barriers and started to believe wholeheartedly in God?

Why am I even unable to begin by renouncing the material things, the transitory and ephemeral? Why, knowing—and knowing, strangely, with humility—my faults, my myriad imperfections, do I go on with outward complacency, yet with growing inward desolation? Why must my mind remain factual, materialist whilst within me I stifle my cry for help and will not yield an iota to the stumbling craving in my soul? Will this rebellion against God never end?

Quos deus vult perdere, prius dementat (Whom the gods wish to destroy, they first make mad). Perhaps this is what is happening to me—or maybe I can seek solace in the thought I am only going through a male menopause.

So this life is only a preparation for the hereafter? This is still an illogical premise to explain the period of human history in which I have lived. The graveyards of Anzio and ten million of the world's finest men swallowed up, sacrificed upon the most incomprehensible of all mankind's bizarre altars—man's inhumanity to man, war.

Twice, three times that number could probably be accounted for, if Russia and China were included. Was it the Sublime purpose to abbreviate for these millions of souls the preparation for the hereafter in anguish and torture? And now we prepare for the unspeakable horrors of yet another war, with weapons which may well portend mankind's final self-destruction.

So Faith is a word the meaning of which eludes me. I mean Faith in the concept of a benign all-seeing God. God, in the sense of a creator, yes. God in the sense of a Supreme Being I can believe in. But a God who believes in me, a God who is aware of my soul's existence, who after death will clear up the great mystery of my reason for life in this world, in this God I have no faith, nor can I begin to seek it with a full heart.

Today, I see a strange world, more bewildering and paradoxical than anything I have read in history, even the birth of Christianity— one half of mankind grimly devoted to the task of stamping out the idea of God and Religion; the other half apathetic to both. Supine and hypocritical, the professed believers in a Christian God today give lipservice in the various totem-houses, listening in private to their priests denounce the other Christian sects with hatred and malice. In the light of the Church's sordid history, its stubborn refusal to keep pace with modern thought, its failure to satisfy the religious needs of today, perhaps this apathy is understandable.

The world's need for Faith is desperate, more desperate than my own, for I am only one lost individual in a tortured universe, a world weary, shocked and shattered. No philosophy, no political fanatical dogma can stand against a true belief in God.

Faith—I wish I had it.

Errol Flynn's last pieces as a writer were about Cuba and Fidel Castro, and they appeared in the *New York Journal-American* in the first week of February 1959. After finishing work on his autobiography, and presumably feeling elated about being a writer again, he proceeded to Cuba to seek out Castro, whose revolutionary ideals intrigued Flynn. Perhaps because he had played them so many times in the movies, Flynn was drawn to political rebels. I suspect that all of his political thinking was along the line of storybook idealism, and with little interest in practical politics.

In going to Cuba, Flynn was probably reliving his trip to the Spanish Civil War in 1937 and there can be little doubt that the Cuban adventure was an attempt at reviving his heroic image of yore, a kind of last fling for Don Quixote Flynn. Later, he appeared in TV talk shows, notably on Jack Paar's, and told of his experiences. By this time, his life was beyond raising any eyebrows. He was simply a "colorful fragment" and a rather sad reminder of former times.

Chapter 4

Success Too Late

The biggest irony in the story of Errol Flynn is that success as a writer came to him posthumously. The recognition he had sought in his early years in Hollywood with his writings, and which soon dwindled into a vain hope, came on a grand scale with his autobiography. He had read and approved all the galleys of *My Wicked, Wicked Ways* and he had every reason to believe it would sell well. It was inevitable that he should write a book about his life. By anybody's yardstick, it had been a complex and colorful life, and he had been making notes on it for years.

In 1957, G.P. Putnam's Sons, New York, gave Flynn a generous advance to write the saga of his life. With his track record as a writer and with a life story more bizarre than that of any other actor in Hollywood, the publisher reckoned it a good gamble. But they did not reckon with his tardiness, nor did they know it was now difficult for him to concentrate on anything for any length of time. Flynn admitted to friends that it was tougher going than he had imagined. That wasn't the only problem.

In Paris in July 1958, Flynn happened to meet Art Buchwald, who wanted to know, as did almost everyone, how the book was coming along. Flynn smiled a little wanly and allowed that he had so far assembled something like fifty thousand words but that he was far from pleased. He told Buchwald, "I lie awake at night plucking at the coverlet wondering what tomorrow's chapter will be. I can't write about myself because I lie to myself. I don't even know they're lies because I believe them. I don't believe in ghost writers. Many of my colleagues who have told all for the right price have less principle about this than I have. I wanted to write the book myself but now I'm willing to give back the advance."

Flynn was not a man noted for giving back money, and Putnam's was not about to let a potential winner slip away. Despite his declaration about having principles, he finally agreed to a ghost writer, albeit on the understanding that the book would appear under Flynn's name, with no mention of a helper. Putnam's hired veteran author and journalist Earl Conrad, who read through all the material Flynn had penned but decided a completely new tack needed to be taken. Late in 1958, Flynn took Conrad with him to his estate in Jamaica and the two men worked together for the next ten weeks. Conrad hired two court stenographers to take down his daily probing and prodding of Flynn—a long, long interview, verging on psycho-analysis. With almost a quarter of a million words of notes, Conrad returned to New York and put together what became known as My Wicked, Wicked Ways. The end product sounded so much like Flynn that few people suspected the hand of another man. And it did indeed become a best-seller.

Looking back on his association with Errol Flynn, Earl Conrad muses, "He was a macrocosm. That is to say he was a convoluted, contradictory enlargement of other men; and through examining him and what had happened to him, you could get insights into the nature of other men, rather like a scientist looking into a microscope at some devilish microbe. It helped me to understand the complicated nature of living as it pertains to all of us. Flynn was a collection of disparate personalities, and he had had too much of everything. Eventually he became a ripped-out-at-the-seams caricature of himself, trying to keep up an image he really didn't want. I noticed he kept no photos of himself and he seemed to avoid looking in mirrors. He told me he would rather have written a few good books than made all his films. Everyone in the world thought they knew Flynn but they didn't—he was isolated by his fame, probably because he was an isolated human being to begin with."

Errol Flynn toward the end of his life found himself with few close friends, partly because he moved about so much, partly because he became bored with people, and largely because he exhausted those around him. "I found that after three or four hours with Errol," says Earl Conrad, "I had to get away from him and be by myself. He was a man on fire—there was so much action and excitement in him."

Flynn was aware of the contradictions of his nature and made many revealing remarks to Conrad for the book, such as, "I want faith, and I am faithless," and "I want to be loved, yet I myself may be incapable of really loving." In Conrad's view, there was also a suicidal streak in Flynn. "He seemed to be an expert on drugs. He told me there were six different ways of killing oneself and that an overdose of morphine was the easiest. One of the things he did for a kick was skin diving, going down eighty and ninety feet. One day, he came rushing up to me after he had just come out of the water and he said, 'My God, what an escape I've just had. My air tank gave out when I was ninety feet down and I don't know how I got up.' He was elated with the exertion, with the excitement of having survived a hassle with death. That gave him a great kick; he lived on that for the rest of the day. That was typical of Flynn."

Flynn stayed in Jamaica after Conrad left. He said he intended to retire from acting within a year or so and live in the new house he was building on his estate near Port Antonio, and even pointed out the spot where he wished to be buried. He also told Conrad that he wanted to form a writing partnership with him and do a number of books together. In the summer of 1959, he went to Hollywood to appear in a TV drama called *The Golden Shanty*. The half-hour playlet, directed by Arthur Hiller, was filmed in three days. Flynn looked like a much older man than fifty—a sick, older man. He had trouble remembering his lines, even in reading them off cue cards. For all that, says Hiller, "He was still a humorous, likable man with a mischievous air about him. But it was painful to look at him now and remember what a graceful athlete he had been only a few years before."

In the first week of October, Flynn made his last appearance before the cameras. He was a guest on *The Red Skelton Show*, playing a gentleman tramp in a comedy sketch. A few days later, he took Beverly Aadland with him to Vancouver, British Columbia, where he intended to discuss the sale of his yacht, the *Zaca*, to a Canadian businessman. A price of $100,000 was agreed upon and Flynn then spent several days being entertained by his hosts. On October 14, while being driven to the airport, he complained of great pains in his back. He asked to see a doctor and his hosts took him to the home of a friend, Dr. Grant A. Gould. The doctor administered a pain-killing drug and Flynn soon felt better, although stiff in the back. His mood picked up and he began telling stories about famous Hollywood personalities. After a while he asked the doctor if he might go to the bedroom and lie down for a while. Because of the stiff back, Dr. Gould advised Flynn to lie on the floor. Beverly covered him with a blanket and his last words were, "See you in an hour." She rejoined the others but decided to look in on Flynn about thirty minutes later. She found him lifeless and a blue-gray color. Dr. Gould shot adrenalin straight into Flynn's heart but neither this nor mouth-to-mouth resuscitation had any effect. Flynn was rushed to a hospital and given oxygen but he failed to respond and he was shortly pronounced dead. His body was shipped to Los Angeles by rail and a few days later he was buried at Forest Lawn—a cemetery he had often decried as ludicrous and one in which he hoped he would not end up. But he received a respectable Episcopal service, with his ex-boss Jack L. Warner delivering a eulogy and his studio colleague Dennis Morgan singing "Home Is the Sailor."

Had Flynn lived to enjoy the success of *My Wicked, Wicked Ways*, which told more than even his most ardent fans expected, he would also have had to do some explaining. There were relatives and friends from the early years, those who had been of help to him, who wondered why they had received no mention. And there were a few people who strongly objected to the manner in which he had portrayed them. Among them were his mother, ex-wife Lili Damita, the Brothers Warner and director Michael Curtiz. These, and others, assailed G.P. Putnam's with protests; consequently *My Wicked, Wicked Ways* appeared in later printings somewhat shorter than the first. Those who had been slighted or ignored reasoned that Flynn in his last year was confused in his recollections and thoughts—a fair assumption in view of the excessive use of drugs and alcohol, particularly so in a man with a propensity for blending fact and fiction. Be that as it may, *My Wicked, Wicked Ways* is a remarkable outpouring of recollections and thoughts. With the help of Earl Conrad, Flynn was able to reveal himself in all his complexity, and with considerable candor. Few public figures have chosen to reveal themselves so intimately and almost none have, or could, tell such tales. If nothing else, Errol Flynn stuffed his fifty years like a huge, bulging bag.

But what of Flynn as a writer? In his book *The Young Errol*, John Hammond Moore gives the opinion that Flynn was an entertaining, highly readable writer, who could probably have made a living as a journalist or short-story writer, had he not become a celebrated actor. But Flynn was lazy. "Why spend time and effort learning a trade or a profession when through wit, physical charm, guile, and theft one could shortcut his way to wealth and ease?" Dr. Moore also believes, as do many who knew Flynn, that he became a victim of his own public image. "Hollywood, the publicity staff at Warner Brothers, and millions of fans who wallowed vicariously in the alleged sexual exploits of this beautiful man created a monster which eventually triumphed over reality." And whatever talent Flynn may have possessed as a writer was an easy victim of that still lingering, phallic, amusing and largely false heroic image. Such an image, such a life, such a man was also victim to almost anything anyone might care to think about him, even that he was capable of espionage and treason.

Chapter 5

Who Was Hermann Erben?

How was Charles Higham able to build up such an impos-
ing charge against Errol Flynn? It takes little examination of *The
Untold Story* to reach the conclusion that the charges are based on
statements of people long dead or those who do not wish to be
identified. Other conclusions on the part of Higham are reached by
inference, supposition, innuendo and strained deduction. But the
basis for the charge of Nazism is Flynn's friendship with an Austrian doctor named Hermann Friedrich Erben. It is more than a
basis; take away Erben and there is nothing left with which to tackle
Flynn in regard to his supposed interest in Nazi Germany.

The core of the charges are contained in the section marked:

Declassified Secret Documents—Espionage—Errol Flynn and Dr. Hermann Friedrich Erben (1926-1968). The section lists 184 documents. Every single one of these documents is about Erben and only five mention Flynn, and in each case he is referred to only as an acquaintance of Erben. Wherever Erben traveled, before, during and after the war, he always let it be known that he had a friend who was a famous movie star. When Erben was arrested in Shanghai after the war, the first thing he said to investigating office Captain Frank Farrell of the OSS was, "Did you know I was Errol Flynn's best friend?"

Flynn was several times interviewed by government officials about Erben and always defended him. Yes, Erben was a wild eccentric, said Flynn, but he thought he had no real political leanings and was not likely to cause any trouble. He was, to use a term of the times, a *screwball*. Had Flynn known more about his crazy chum he might have been more cautious with his protection. But how much did Flynn know? And who was this man Erben?

According to Charles Higham, "Dr. Hermann Friedrich Erben was one of the most important and ingenious Nazi agents of the twentieth century." He was nothing of the kind. In the history of the Nazi regime, Erben is a figure of no consequence, and had it not been for his friendship with a famous movie star his name would mean nothing. He was an ardent admirer of Adolf Hitler, which hardly made him unique in the Thirties, and after the German annexation of Austria in 1938, he became a card carrying Nazi Party member, as did most Austrian professionals. No doctor, lawyer, journalist or musician was likely to find employment without such a card. Just how dedicated he was to the Nazi cause is difficult to assess since he was a man who changed his tune with the times and bent the truth in any direction that suited the argument.

Erben was born in Vienna in 1897 and it was in his native city that he died eighty-seven years later. However, not many of those years were actually spent in Austria. His travels were prodigious. Erben roamed the world as a ship's doctor and held many posts in far-flung places in the Middle East, Asia and the Far East, eventually winning some distinction as a specialist in tropical diseases. Despite his epic amount of travel on all the continents and oceans of the world, his life is not difficult to research because Erben kept meticulous diaries all his life. He also kept every ship, train and plane ticket he ever bought, in addition to amassing tens of thousands of photographs. He was an avid photographer. In his last years of life, his apartment in Vienna was crammed with boxes containing all the papers and pictures he had collected, along with other boxes in a basement storage room. Additionally, there are massive amounts of documentation available on Erben due to the investigations made of him by various American government departments.

Erben served with the Austrian Army in the first World War and was demobilized with the rank of first lieutenant. He then enrolled as a student at the School of Medicine at the University of Vienna, from which he won a scholarship to study metabolic research in America. Soon after his arrival in New York in early 1924, he let it be known that he wished to register for eventual American citizenship. In the summer of 1926, he returned to Vienna to complete the studies necessary for his license as a doctor, and after two months, he returned to New York, where he passed a State Civil Service examination as a qualified medical doctor. Accompanied by his wife, Erben worked as a doctor at the Wards Island State Hospital before he accepted a position with the Pacific Institute of Tropical Medicine, which took him to San Francisco. It was in that city on November 10, 1930, that Hermann Erben received his papers as an American citizen. Except for the allowed return visit to Vienna, he had, so he claimed, lived the requisite unbroken amount of time in the United States to qualify. But he did not reveal that he had spent much of 1929 on a scientific mission in North Queensland for the Australian government. That unreported period of time would have disqualified him—and it would be the first of many devious doings which would cause problems for Erben with the American government.

In his book *American Swastika* (Doubleday, 1985), Charles Higham states, "Dr. Erben was born a Jew in Vienna and later abandoned his people to become a member of the SA, the most fanatical branch of the SS, and later the SD and the Abwehr." This confusion of the SA with the SS is a considerable error to be made by anyone purporting to deal with the history of Nazism. The SA (Sturmabteilung—Storm Troopers) were the loutish brown shirts who gradually became an embarrassment to Hitler. In 1934, the Fuehrer, in order to consolidate his power, allowed the rival SS (Schutzstaffel—Guard Detachments) to purge the leadership of the SA. This included the murder of its commander, Ernst Röhm. It seems highly unlikely that a Viennese medical student, especially one bent on an American scholarship, would join the ranks of the SA, particularly in view of the fact that the SA was not operative in Austria at that time.

The SD (Sicherheitsdienst—Security Service) was a tightly organized branch of the SS, presided over by the brilliant but barbarous Reinhardt Heydrich, who like all his colleagues was virtually anti-Semetic. With Jewish blood, Hermann Erben had about as much chance of becoming a member of the SS as Martin Luther King, Jr. would have had being elected an officer in the Ku Klux Klan. Erben did, however, become an informer for the Abwehr (Military Intelligence) in Mexico City in January 1941, at a time when he had departed forever the company of Errol Flynn.

Having attained American citizenship, Hermann Erben proceeded to live almost everywhere but in the United States. The new American was sent by the Pacific Institute of Tropical Medicine, located at the Unversity of California in Berkeley, to South America for a year. After that, he began the first of many assignments as a ship's doctor, joining the Dollar Line and serving on the *President Garfield*. At the end of 1932, Erben accepted another posting for scientific research, this one taking him to New Guinea, which is where young Errol Flynn comes into the picture.

Flynn and Erben met on April 14, 1933, at Salamaua, New

Guinea, when Flynn boarded the German freighter *Friderun*— Flynn bound for England to seek life as an actor, and Erben on the way back to Vienna to assume post graduate medical studies. It seems to have been a case of fascination at first sight for both of them. The bizarre personality Erben, a man of many experiences, much knowledge and many loudly expressed opinions, became a kind of mentor to the young man, who in turn probably struck Erben as a likely kindred spirit. In the years to come, Erben would win few friends and draw much comment as a man of obnoxious behavior. Be that as it may, when Flynn came to write *My Wicked, Wicked Ways*, he credited Erben as the man who gave him a sense of style. "This man was the great influence of my life. He showed me in a humorous, bawdy, Rabelaisian, tough, rough way the difference between a man with no soul and a man with one, even though neither of us was sure what a soul was . . . he showed me the complete irrelevance of the existence that we humans have while on earth . . . from him I learned to laugh at the worst disasters."

The characters, the souls, of Errol Flynn and Hermann Erben would come in for some questioning over the following years but their loyalty to each other as friends was firm. Flynn always spoke up for his strange Austrian buddy, and to the day he died, Erben maintained that Flynn was his dearest, most understanding friend —and that Flynn was never involved in espionage.

Flynn and Erben spent more than two months getting to Europe, and had a whale of a time doing it. They changed ships in Hong Kong and sailed for Colombo, in what was then known as Ceylon, aboard a French freighter, the *D'Artagnan*. By way of the Suez Canal, that vessel reached Marseilles on June 20, the day of Flynn's twenty-fourth birthday. He proceeded to London via Paris and Erben got to Vienna on June 23, where he put in a year of medical studies. In 1934, Erben was appointed the medical officer of the Austro-American Trans-Asiatic Expedition, leading the team by car through Palestine, Iraq and Iran, then via the Khyber Pass into India, and finally through Burma and Indochina to Peking. The following year, he ended up in New York—making a brief but necessary visit to his newly adopted country—but soon afterwards embarked on another medical expedition to South America.

Although Errol Flynn has gone down in Hollywood history as a great adventurer and traveler, his achievements very nearly pale when compared to friend Erben. The two saw each other for the first time since Marseilles when Erben turned up in Los Angeles on September 19, 1936. Flynn was now a movie star involved in the making of his fifth film, *Another Dawn*, and he was able to entertain Erben in a royal manner. After ten days together, during which time Erben managed to offend a good many people with his apparently arrogant manners, the itinerant doctor embarked from Los Angeles for the Panama Canal, then via Cuba to Buenos Aires, in his capacity as the medical officer of the American ship SS *West Mahwah*. The captain of that vessel was puzzled by the fact that Erben took hundreds of photos of every port through which they passed and reported the matter to the American Consul in Pernambuco, Brazil, who in turn submitted a report to the Secretary of State in Washington. No one could decide if the ship's doctor was an agent of a foreign power or simply an ovelry enthusiastic amateur photographer, but from that point onwards, Erben was marked as a man on whom an eye had best be kept.

Much of the FBI and other government department documentation on Erben relates more to his problems with travel than to espionage. In point of fact, prior to his official signing on with the Abwehr in 1941, there is only scant evidence of his turning in of reports to the Nazi government. Most of his problems stemmed from his high-handed disregard for obtaining proper travel documents. As a ship's doctor and as a doctor on foreign postings, he needed to constantly inform the American government of his movements, and obtain permissions. Apparently he failed to do so, and apparently he bamboozled his way around the world on the strength of his seamanship and medical papers. Because of this, much of the

Erben documentation lies with the State Department and the Immigration and Naturalization Service rather than the FBI.

Erben had what appears to have been contempt for official travel papers, which is at variance with his stated admiration for the Nazis, whose own fervor for precise documentation was Germanic in the extreme. As an American citizen, he could be much more lax than as a member of the Third Reich. Erben was also, by the mid-Thirties, a marked man due to his carrying of drugs. As a doctor in and out of many ports, he had reason to carry medical drugs but suspicions arose that he was also peddling narcotics. Whether true or not—and he always denied it—it would have made him a woeful espionage agent, a job which requires that the agent do nothing to put himself in a questionable light.

Erben's capriciousness, his irreverence for official ways and means was one of the things Flynn admired about his Austrian friend. Flynn's own nature was of this kind and it was surely abetted by knowing Erben. However, that disregard for proper methods would soon cause Flynn a little discomfort.

Following a medical assignment in South America, Erben resurfaced in Los Angeles on February 11, 1937, and descended on Flynn. Erben was in trouble once again with the INS and spent several days being examined regarding his passport and visas. With that mess cleared up Erben then proposed making a trip with Flynn—a fun trip, an adventure, something of the kind they had shared four years previous: A trip to Spain to see what the civil war was all about.

Chapter 6

The Spanish Fling

In *Errol Flynn: The Untold Story*, Charles Higham makes much of the Flynn-Erben trip to Spain, citing it as Flynn's first overt attempt to aid the Nazi cause and assist an agent who would become an enemy of Britain and America in the coming World War.

The alacrity with which Flynn picked up on Erben's suggestion that they take off for Spain is not hard to imagine. By now, he had been a movie star for two years, and much as he enjoyed the money and the lifestyle, he was also starting to complain about being overworked by Jack L. Warner and his brothers. Warners in that period was a well administered film factory whose employees quipped about it being a penitentiary. Be that as it may, it was one hordes of unemployed actors and artisans would willingly have broken into. But Flynn had made five films, one after the other, and he wanted a break. He also wanted to get away from his wife.

Flynn met Lili Damita on the ship that brought him to America and he married her in June of 1935, just before he was given the lead in *Captain Blood*. Their professional lives were now about to go in opposite directions. Damita, eight years older than Flynn, had been a film star in her native France and also had a goodly list of Hollywood pictures to her credit. Her career was in decline at this time, and once she married Flynn she retired from acting. And once he was seen as *Captain Blood,* Flynn ceased being a nonentity and stepped into overnight stardom.

Many years later, Jack Warner mused, "I wonder if The Baron, as I called him, would have turned down that chance if he could have foreseen the sordid and troublesome road ahead. I doubt it. He had to live as he lived." Warner and Flynn enjoyed a bantering relationship over the years, sometimes a little loud, especially when it came to money, but mostly they joshed. Warner, whose lifestyle was almost as proper as that of an Oxford don, seemed to have more of a fondness for Flynn than most of the actors on his payroll. Perhaps he saw, as did so many others, something in the flamboyant actor that he envied. Certainly no one has summed up the Flynn appeal better than Warner: "To the Walter Mittys of the world he was all the heroes in one magnificent, sexy, animal package."

Lili Damita probably understood that appeal better than anyone. She loved him intensely, but she knew she would not be able to hang on to him, much as she tried. At the party following the premiere of *Captain Blood*, Flynn was showered with compliments, which he relished. His wife did not. Delmer Daves, then a writer and later a director, was among the guests. He spotted Damita at one point in tears. "She said, 'Tonight I have lost my husband.' I suppose it did happen that night—for when Errol arrived, boisterously happy, exultant, it was easy to see he meant to enjoy this brave new world that brought him stardom that night. And he did."

Lili Damita was a feisty woman, quick of temper and according to Flynn "pathologically jealous." Their marriage staggered through seven years with endless fights—they were called The Battling

Flynns—and there were periods of separation, the most famous being one of several months in 1938 when Flynn and David Niven shared a house which became known as Cirrhosis-by-the-Sea. Flynn was clearly not a man with any need at this time in his life to be married, indeed as husband material he was a spectacularly poor choice, but Lili, whose occasional ferocity caused Flynn to dub her Tiger Lil, hung on. In her tantrums, she hit him with anything at hand and he often turned up for work with abrasions. She disliked most of his friends, especially Hermann Erben, whom she called "a pig!"

Erben's suggestion that they go to Spain probably hit Flynn like a load of catnip thrown at a cat. Not only would it be a flirtation with danger, but it would be one he could write about. His first book, *Beam Ends*, had just come out and he also had a few magazine articles to his credit. With these under his belt, he easily got a commission from the Hearst Press. The Higham charges that Erben could never have gotten into Spain without Flynn are undeniable. Spain was off limits to most Americans wanting to go there as visitors, and with Erben's record as a naturalized citizen who failed to spend the requisite periods in the United States deemed necessary to support his citizenship, and his failure to make accurate reports, he had little chance of setting foot in the country. On the other hand, when a popular, handsome movie actor brings his charm and influence to bear, things can usually be arranged. Erben would go in as Flynn's photographer and as such he would indeed serve.

Politically, Flynn was a man of little firm persuasion. If anything he leaned to the left. The first I heard of this was from David Niven. I initially met Niven at MGM in 1968 when he was filming *The Impossible Years*. I had gone to see him to record his Flynn impressions for my documentary, *Requiem for a Cavalier*, and it was during that meeting that he said something that has been widely quoted since: "One marvelous thing about Errol was you always knew where you were with him because he always let you down." Niven smiled after that and added, "I'm painting a black picture of him. He was a good friend as a matter of fact. Errol was a many-sided creature and he was a great man for the little guy. He was always charging into the offices of the Brass at Warner Brothers and making tremendous scenes about people he thought were being badly treated in the lower echelons."

A trip to Europe met with Lili's approval, but when she found out Erben was going, she opted to fly ahead and meet Flynn in Paris. Flynn and Erben sailed from New York on the *Queen Mary* on February 24 and arrived in Southampton on March 1. Flynn spent two weeks in London and Erben left for a quick visit to Berlin. Just what he did there is unclear, but he might well have checked in with the Gestapo to inform them of his impending Spanish visit, with an offer to keep his eyes open for those German leftists fighting with the Loyalists. Hitler had supplied Franco with a vast amount of aid by sending his Condor Legion of army and air force units, and he was enraged by the idea of Germans joining the International Brigade in opposition. As an admirer of Hitler and a fellow anti-communist, Erben might well have volunteered his services. However, this is an assumption on my part, just as I am assuming he told Flynn nothing about this side of his affairs. Hermann was a devious, crafty kind of man, and his movie star chum was still quite a bit the naïve colonial.

Flynn spent a total of ten days in Spain, and just how much spying a man can do in a foreign country in that period of time is open to question, especially if he has press coverage and goes around giving autographs. He got to Barcelona on March 26, where he spent the next six days, much of it in the company of the Warner Brothers staff at their Barcelona office. Newspaper coverage of the time shows him in the Warner offices, on the steps of the building with a crowd of fans, sitting in sidewalk cafes, visiting a hospital and various monuments, and generally behaving like a celebrity tourist. He and Erben also went to the Ministry of Propaganda, where they were supplied with a car and driver in order to make their subsequent tour. Photos also reveal that the doors of the car were lettered: GENERALITAT DE CATALUNYA—COMMISSARIAT DE PROPAGANDA. Since all of the touring was done in the company of a Loyalist staff driver, the Higham charges of Flynn being engaged in espionage seem limp.

Flynn and Erben set off for Valencia on March 31, with most of the day spent driving down the coastal road. They spent two nights at the Hotel Victoria and visited the International Brigade at Albacete on May 1. The following day they left for Madrid, where they spent three nights at the Hotel Gran Via. They spent all of Saturday, May 3, visiting the front lines at Guadalajara, where they seemingly saw no action. Madrid was under artillery fire during the time they were there, and at some point, Flynn was hit on the head by a piece of flying brick and knocked unconscious, or so he claimed. Erben then filed a press report that the famous movie star had been killed, or so he claimed. Be that as it may, Flynn decided to pack his bags by the end of the day. He attended a party at the hotel in the evening — Ernest Hemingway and author Sidney Franklin were also in attendance—which went on until two in the morning. Flynn left four hours later, driving first to Barcelona and then flying back to Paris. Erben stayed on.

That Flynn apparently left in a hurry had much to do with Erben. Charles Higham claims that the two men got into Spain by claiming that they were bringing in a million dollars of Hollywood money to help the Loyalists. I believe Flynn's own version is the more likely. He had become suspicious of the degree of civility and assistance he had been given by the Loyalist officials. He found out why on the final day when his driver asked, "When are you going to give us the money?" Erben started to laugh and admitted that the ruse had been his. According to Flynn, Erben then explained, "What I wanted was a chance to operate, to work and operate, that's all. The only way I could do it and get by in style here was to use you." Flynn replied, "Thank you, Comrade Sonofabitch!"

News of the Flynn "death" was flashed around the world by the press, which made excellent publicity, but not of a kind that pleased

Jack Warner, who did not want his star showing favor with either side in the Spanish conflict lest it have bearing upon box office returns. He also wired Flynn to get back to California as soon as possible.

Erben stayed in Spain and worked as a field surgeon for the British Red Cross in the Loyalist sector, although taking a lot of photos that he later admitted sending to Berlin. Higham claims that Flynn was given thirteen spools of film, which he then turned over to a Nazi agent in Paris. Again, no evidence. The reels were shots of Flynn which he needed to illustrate the articles he wanted to write. An entry in Erben's diary of some months later reveals that Flynn sent back to him ten spools of the films.

Had Flynn actually been involved in espionage in Spain, it would have surfaced long ago in the plethora of memoirs and histories written by people who took part in the Spanish Civil War and in Second World War intelligence activities. Ex-Nazi intelligence agents have been prolific in writing about their adventures. The involvement of a famous Hollywood personality would have been impossible to suppress.

Flynn apparently enjoyed his Spanish fling, although comment came from some quarters that going there and deriving publicity from it was not in the best of taste. The most bitter comments came from the reporters who were suckered into the false story of his being wounded in action and subsequently dying. Was this one of the perversely humored Dr. Erben's practical jokes or was Flynn party to it? No one will ever know.

In his book *Bullfighter from Brooklyn* (Prentice-Hall, 1952), Sidney Franklin recalls his meeting with Flynn in Madrid. Flynn had turned to him for help because Franklin was acquainted with Lili Damita. Flynn wanted to know if Franklin could help him take a trip through the Franco lines. "I explained the chances he would have to take. He might get shot. Couldn't I arrange it so he could get through safely tonight? I suggested that he go back to Valencia, catch a boat to Gibraltar, and go in that way. But he didn't want to do that. He only wanted to go through the lines and he wanted to go that night. When I explained that no one could guarantee his safety while going through the lines, he dropped the subject."

That night, Franklin joined Flynn for a farewell party in his suite in the Gran Via Hotel and then saw Flynn off early the next morning on the outskirts of Madrid, "I explained the road to his chauffeur... and went back to bed." A few hours later, he was awakened by newsmen wanting to know about Flynn's condition—was it true he had been shot trying to get through the lines? Erben had given them some particulars but nobody seemed to know if Flynn was alive or dead. "Every capital in the world was frantic for details of the disaster." Franklin explained that he had just seen Flynn off. He next called various check points along the route Flynn was taking back to Barcelona and confirmed that the actor was safely on his way.

The least favorable comment on this Flynn adventure is contained in *The Autobiography of a Spanish Woman* (Harcourt, Brace, 1939) by Constancia de la Mora, who was with the censor's office of the Loyalist Ministry of Propaganda at the time. "He came into the Press Office at a moment when we were harrowingly busy, demanded a motor car, permits, passes, guides, and the like, to go to Madrid. We were very short of gasoline, every drop counted. The regular correspondents were trying to defer their business trips until we got a new supply of petrol. But Mr. Errol Flynn could not wait; his time was too valuable. So he departed for Madrid with our precious gasoline in his tanks." De la Mora went on to say that her office was thrown into chaos with the news that Flynn had been wounded and perhaps killed. She regretted not having the opportunity to meet him again. "We would have really liked to have told him our opinion of his conduct, conduct peculiar under any circumstances, but most remarkable, if that is the word, at a time when men were dying for liberty all around him."

When de la Mora's book was published, Flynn was incensed and moved to take legal action against her. He was wisely advised not to do so.

Charles Higham has chosen to see the Flynn fling in Spain in the darkest hues. He is, of course, entitled to any view he wishes but he is on shaky legal grounds when he alters a government document to prove his points. Higham's changes in an FBI document were discovered by William Donati while preparing the book *My Days With Errol Flynn* (Roundtable, 1989), written by Flynn's longtime friend and stunt double Buster Wiles, for whom Donati was a literary collaborator, and to which book Donati gave in the appendix his own rebuttal to the Higham-Flynn charges.

The document in question is dated January 29, 1944, and concerns an FBI *Espionage—G2—Registration Act* report on a Spaniard, Carlos Vejarano Y Cassina, suspected of Nazi involvement during the Second World War. In the report, the Spaniard refers to meeting Hermann Erben in Berlin in May of 1937, in company with Antonio Vargas, Vejarano's contact agent. In *The Untold Story*, Higham uses this report but advises he has "slightly condensed it." What he has also done is take out names and replace them with blanks, presumably to give the document a greater air of mystery. No blanks are visible in the actual document. The alterations occur at three points in the Higham interpretation. Here are the excerpts, with the operative words in italics:

1. *The FBI Document*:
   VARGAS explained that this German had just completed a tour of the various Spanish fronts in company with ERROL FLYNN, the movie actor, *and had taken* numerous pictures of gun establishments and military objectives in *"Red"* Spain. These pictures lay in a huge pile on Vargas' desk.
   The Higham version:
   (Blank) explained that this German had just completed a tour of the various fronts in company with Errol Flynn and *they* had taken numerous pictures of gun establishments and military objectives

in *Loyalist* Spain. These pictures lay in a huge pile on (Blank)'s desk.

2. *The FBI document:*

   One of the German military officials had called the Embassy advising that they were sending this man over in order that members of the Spanish Embassy in Berlin who were at that time superiors of General Franco, could view the pictures that their *agent* had taken in Spain with a view that this might help the Franco forces.

   The Higham version of the above is the same except that the word *agent* becomes *agents*.

3. *The FBI document*:

   VEJARANO advised that he had looked through these pictures and noticed several pictures of the German in the company of ERROL FLYNN and the various military objectives *the German* had photographed.

   The Higham version:

   (Blank) advised that he had looked through these pictures and noticed several pictures of the German with Errol Flynn and the various military objectives which *he* had photographed.

These simple but deft word changes place Flynn in a dubious and false light. Clearly the agent-photographer is Erben, and while he presented some shots he had taken of Flynn in Loyalist Spain, the bulk were later taken on Franco's side of the line.

The truth about this bizarre episode in Flynn's life might well have been summed up by Erben when he told Joseph Fegerl in Vienna in 1985, at a time when Fegerl was putting together a book of Erben's photos, "Flynn was never wounded. The whole Spanish trip with him was a publicity tour, assisted by Warner Bros., the Catalunya Comissariat de Propaganda and the press." Be that as it may, Flynn's Spanish fling was soon forgotten and nothing came of his plan to write a series of articles for the Hearst Press. He complained that no one seemed interested in his sympathy for the Loyalist cause and concern over Hitler's aid to Franco. Why should they have been? Professional reporters were filling the pages of the world's newspapers with plenty of much more credible coverage. Flynn had to settle for a single article in the July 1937 issue of *Photoplay*.

WHAT REALLY HAPPENED TO ME IN SPAIN*

I am quite dead.

I am quite a bit surprised about it, too. Struck me all of a heap, so to speak, when I found out about it. For three weeks I've had to argue with people—try to prove that I'm not some new kind of a zombie. The best authorities between Madrid and Hollywood have all concurred that I'm not. I don't exist. I got killed. And, what's more, they seem to have a cheated look when I show up and start talking.

When I crossed back into France from Spain, a little rolly-polly French reporter gazed at me indignantly.

"Mais M'sieur est mort! I have written so! All over the world M'sieur is dead and now M'sieur returns alive!"

He was really quite wrought up about it and somehow I felt I owed him an apology. I suppose I really should have been dead, but when you get right down to it, I just didn't feel like leaving this vale of tear-gas bombs at the moment—the last few weeks having been so crammed with action and excitement. The events leading up to my extremely sad death were more than a bit exciting in themselves.

When Jack Warner said I could have eight weeks off, I left so fast he couldn't change his mind, grab a phone and have me back for portrait stills. Somehow, I couldn't imagine the publicity department following me into the front line trenches of a nice healthy war. It makes publicity men and producers very nervous to be shot at. So I picked on Spain for a few weeks rest and quiet.

Arriving in Spain, I felt I was right back in *The Charge of the Light Brigade*. After having passed through better than fifty "Committees," I arrived at the famous old Grand Via Hotel in Madrid.

Photoplay, July 1937. Copyright *Photoplay*. Reprinted from *From a Life of Adventure: The Writings of Errol Flynn* (Lyle Stuart, 1980).

Flynn the author, writing *Beam Ends* in 1936. (Basil Courtel Collection)

Making his first visit to Hollywood, Hermann Erben with Flynn on the set of *Another Dawn* at Warner Bros. on September 25, 1936.

In Barcelona on March 31, 1937, setting out on a three-day tour of the Spanish Civil War, courtesy of the Propaganda Ministry of Catalunya, who provided the car and a chauffeur (above) and visiting the members of the International Brigade at Albacete on April 1, 1937. Hermann Erben is at left in second row. (Both Copyright: Josef Fegerl)

The quintessential Flynn film image. *The Adventures of Robin Hood* (1938), with Patric Knowles as Will Scarlett.

While making *Santa Fe Trail* in 1940, Olivia de Havilland said it was the first time she noticed Flynn showing signs of jealousy when other men showed her attention, including Ronald Reagan.

At the peak of the Flynn good life; aboard his ketch *Sirocco* (named after the old one in Australia) in 1939, the only year he was among the Top Ten at the box office, and having a whale of a life off screen.

1939 was also the year his family visited him in America for the first time. Sister Rosemary, mother Marelle and the esteemed Professor Theodore Thomson Flynn. (Rick Dodd Collection)

The only politician Flynn idolized was Franklin Roosevelt, here with Eleanor at a horse show in Washington, D.C., in 1939. Flynn rode their entry in the show and afterwards took home an autographed photo of the President. (Rick Dodd Collection)

On board the aircraft carrier *Enterprise* while making *Dive Bomber* in 1941, with Ralph Bellamy (above) and with director Michael Curtiz. It was the last time Flynn and Curtiz worked together, the actor claiming the director was a brutal taskmaster who cared nothing for Flynn safety and comfort.

On trial in Los Angeles in January of 1943 on charges of statutory rape, with his masterly lawyer Jerry Giesler. Walking behind Flynn is one of the two girls involved, Peggy Satterlee. (Rick Dodd Collection)

Doing his song-and-dance routine in the all-star *Thank Your Lucky Stars* (1943), playing a Cockney cadging drinks from bartender Monte Blue and claiming epic war victories. Flynn enjoyed spoofing his heroic screen image and like all the other stars in the film donated his salary to service charities. (Paul James Collection)

Pretending to conduct the WAC Band at Fort Meade, Kansas, in 1943, one of Flynn's trips to entertain the services. (Rick Dodd Collection)

"Committees," incidentally, are small patrols of men, armed to the teeth, who examine your credentials while their rifle muzzles probe at your fifth rib. You may have the right papers, but they always look at you as though you stole them.

I was glad of the comparative peace of the hotel and immediately took a nice, cheap room on the third floor with a lovely view.

At nine-thirty the next morning, I found out why it was so cheap. If you've spent the last twenty hours riding over shell-pitted roads at eighty m.p.h., you rather like to lie abed for a while the next morning, so I was in no mood for levity when awakened by a sibilant whooshing, followed by a loud crash. I muttered something about somebody please let the dogs out and I tried to get back to sleep. At that moment, there came another loud whoosh-bang, and I was suddenly uncomfortably aware that I wasn't back in Hollywood, so it couldn't be the dogs.

I opened a tentative eye and peered through the window. A few yards away, bathed in the morning sunlight, stood the huge Telephone Building. But something was wrong with it. It had holes in it. Large, gaping holes. And from one of them, dust, bricks and debris were at that moment still falling. I was pondering this unusual phenomenon when, directly overhead, another whooshing sound approached, banged off and there, before my eyes, was still another brand new hole in the Telephone Company's lovely building.

I rose and left my bed rapidly.

In fact, I didn't even wait for the elevator. My pal, Doctor Erben, and I swooped down three flights of stairs with an ease that would drive a trapeze artist to an early, brooding grave. Arriving in the lobby, we wrapped ourselves in bathrobes and dignity and approached the clerk.

"Buenos dias," he smiled. "I trust that you have slept well and are over your fatigue. The accommodations are excellent but, of course, the service—" he shrugged—"La Guerra!"

We agreed that the service was a bit hampered by the good old guerra and that the view was indeed excellent. The clerk expressed polite interest when we informed him that the view had three spanking new holes in it. He glanced at his watch.

"Ah, yes, to be sure! Nine forty-five. It is that way every morning. The enemy warm up their guns with three shells at the Telephone Building every morning. You may return to your rooms now in complete safety. There will be no more bombardment until tomorrow morning at the same hour—excepting, of course, strays. But they won't be intentional."

Erben cleared his throat and mentioned something about quieter rooms anyway. They could be had, but they cost three times as much. They were in the cellar and the view was very bad. We hastened to assure him that we would readily sacrifice the view of the sorely wounded Telephonica and in a few moments were installed in the crowded but capacious cellars of the Grand Via Hotel along with dozens of war correspondents, soldiers and Government officials. Off duty, they used the common rooms of the basement for quiet drinks, billiards and a rousing game of dominoes at the table near the furnace. They turned out to be a grand bunch of guys who took life easy and very, very lightly. In their business, they have to!

With their help, it was only a few hours before we had our *salvoconductos* (safe conduct passes) in order and an armed guide and car driver assigned to us. It is really a strange thing to see an embattled city, under bombardment half the time, continuing its business more or less as usual. The men on the street cars, going to and from their regular work, don't even look up from their daily papers as the shells howl overhead. It wasn't long before we felt much the same way, hardly even turning to look when a twelve-incher split the air. One thing that I never did get over, though, was the chilling and deadly staccato bark of the machine guns.

But all the guns and bombs in Spain frightened me only half as much as Pedro. Pedro was a dark, sleepy-eyed little Spaniard who wore an outsized revolver at the ready even when he went to bed. He piloted us around Madrid and the front sectors with unquenchable ardor. He had a habit of driving at 120 kilometers an hour over bad roads and turning around to the back seat for a friendly chat at the same time. When I add that he had the Spanish habit of talking with his hands, you'll see what I mean.

He must have had an extra eye in the back of his head. I would see a large shell hole dead ahead but would be ashamed to mention it. I'd done that so often before. I'd sit there and feel myself going pale with horror as we roared on towards it, without any slacking in speed. Just as disaster seemed inevitable, Pedro would take a casual glance at the road, see the hole and, with one hand, swerve expertly around it on two wheels and return to the conversation—all without batting an eye. Once, coming back from the Guadalajara front, we heard a plane approaching, looked out and saw a huge tri-motored bomber swooping down over the road. Pedro stepped on it!

If we'd thought we'd been travelling before, we then found out how Pedro could really dynamite along when he put his mind to it. He kept the car careening from side to side to make a more difficult target for the machine gunners above. Just as I was about to feel I'd rather be bombed than drive on like this, Pedro jammed on his brakes. The car immediatley turned around twice in its tracks like a top. We wrenched open the doors and dove headlong into a ditch. A few seconds later, the plane roared overhead, a single burst of machine gun fire cutting a neat dotted line down the length of the automobile. A few minutes later, that same plane dropped hell and fury on an airdrome near Albacite.

Back at the hotel, we really felt the need of a few Malagas with the boys. It was then that we heard tell of one of the war's most fascinating scenes—the front lines at night. We'd been up and all through the University City front in the daytime. The passes were devilishly difficult to wrangle and we were told that night passes were frankly impossible. We had, however, our night and day passes for the Madrid front proper and, when I caught an answering gleam in Erben's eye, I knew that sooner or later Erben and Flynn would be watching the fireworks at night on the front.

If I'd known what was in store for us then, I have an idea that at least one Irish actor would have gone to his grave without ever having seen the fascinating horror and repellant beauty of spouts of flame belching into a velvet night while the drums of war resounded in a crashing, menacing crescendo.

As soon as darkness fell, we started. Once outside the hotel, we were stopped every block or two by a "Committee" who suspiciously examined our passes. There are no lights in Madrid at night and you make your way by the aid of extremely dim flashlights. One bright enough to really see by would land its owner in jail at the first corner. The black silence of the city at night is enough to make your hair stand on end. Very occasionally a dim, firefly-like glow slowly moving down a street will warn you of another pedestrian. Hurriedly, silently, you pass, holding your breath. Suddenly out of nowhere, you hear a swift movement, the metallic triple-click of a carbine and a barked command—"Alto!" Believe me, you alto. It isn't healthy to even twitch an eyelid after that blunt order to halt.

A lot of those "Committees" think it saves time to ask the questions afterwards. Slowly, your heart in your mouth, you make your way through the bitterly cold streets. It seemed forever and a day before we reached the limit of the patrols, crawled past the picket line and into the depopulated area just behind the front where night passes don't do you any good.

At that point, it was necessary to slide along, cautiously flattened against walls, ducking into cavernous doorways, squirming over loose piles of incredible filth and debris, guided only by the increasing volume of sound from the firing lines. It must have taken us a full hour to cover a distance of not more than five or six hundred yards—and every yard is indelibly in my memory. Scared? Of course I was! But I wouldn't have missed it for a million, cash in hand. However, the real kick lay ahead.

About the time when I was beginning to think that the rest of my life would be spent flat on my belly crawling, scrambling, running and dodging through impenetrable blackness, a blackness so dense it made you feel almost dizzy, we came to a corner.

"The Rosales!" whispered Erben.

Once the gayest and proudest plaza of all Madrid, the Rosales is now a shambles of gutted buildings. In place of music, song and laughter, all you hear there now in the line of music is the tenor of machine guns and the bass of heavy artillery.

It was impossible to go any further. Although the lines were dead ahead, most of the actual combat was going on about a quarter of a mile down to our right. From where we stood, we could look obliquely along the lines, get a full view of the fighting. Both in sound and vision, the whole scene was a little like a symphony coming up from lulls into arpeggios and rising into earth shaking fortissimos. It was staggering and a bit bewildering to realize that human beings were down there trying to kill and maim men they'd never seen, had nothing against—blindly killing under orders for a cause they hardly understood, if anyone does understand those things at all.

There is no cover across the wide Rosales, and a few hundred yards away a machine gunner sent blasts of flame and lead whipping across every few seconds. A little further along was the concealed emplacement of large caliber guns firing at minute intervals. Concealed, that is, by day. By night the Rosales is lit up for fifty yards as the orange flash jumps from the muzzle. Almost immediately, from across the valley a couple of kilometers away, would come the answering flash from the opposing artillery position. Nearly a full second would elapse after we saw the flash before hearing the dull boom and then the whine of the shell as it hurtled overhead into the heart of the city.

Erben and I took shelter, such as it was, around the corner of a ruined building, only half of which was left standing. That particular spot had once been heavily contested and blasted into debris, but as far as we knew, no shells had landed there for about two weeks. Therefore, we felt as safe as possible that close to the lines.

We weren't.

Erben had brought along his camera to take some night shots and was just closing up the equipment, preparatory to starting the long squirm back to a drink and a cigarette. I took a last look at the lines. Across the valley, I saw the now familiar flash, waited for the boom and the whine.

It came. But this time the whine sounded different. Closer it came. Closer! Paralyzed, I suddenly knew that this one wasn't headed into town. Erben opened his mouth to yell, but no sound issued. The whine became an incredible shriek...

I'll never know whether some spontaneous muscular convulsion or the concussion of the shell itself threw us flat, but whatever the agency, it is to that we owe our lives. We landed on the ground, nearly unconscious. The shattered wreck of the wall at our backs was a tottery shield, but it worked. In the split second before I lost consciousness, I heard the sickening sound of shrapnel smacking up against the brick with a sound like fifty eggs cracking on a footpath...

When I came to, someone had, I was sure, inserted a singularly unpleasant and painful baseball between my skull and scalp. There were lights all around and I couldn't quite make out if the pearly gates now had neon signs instead of pearls, or if it were actually the cubicle in the basement of the Grand Via that we had inhabited for a couple of weeks. I was about to make some angry remark to Erben, to stop him from swimming about the ceiling that way, when he alit of his own volition, grinned and asked me how I felt. I told him. I can't tell you—not in print, anyway.

All that had happened, fortunately, was that a large chunk of plaster had been jarred loose from the building by the concussion of the shell. It had dropped like a large sombrero on top of my crown from a height of twenty or thirty feet and laid me out for about four hours. I still get headaches, and I'll be much more careful about walking under ladders in the future.

As I started to feel a little more alive, I began to be faintly and modestly proud of my war wounds until my Spanish confreres gazed dispassionately at them in the bar and passed them off as mere scratches. Scratch, indeed! It was my head and it hurt like hell!

It wasn't until I got to Paris that someone of the French press told me I had been dead for some days. Naturally, I appreciated the notion and then rushed around to send off much-alive wires to the parents in Ireland and telephone my small French pal in London.

She was so relieved at learning the Master's person was all in one piece, she ran me up a telephone bill which looked in French francs like Einstein's Theory! By the way, she got a telegram during that period which she insists on having framed.

She says it will serve me as a reminder any time I begin to get the urge to return to the wars.

It's a strange feeling to read a sympathetic little note written about yourself from someone else.

It starts:

"In this hour of your sadness we want you to know how we feel for you over the loss of Errol. We feel sure that his death will not . . ."

Try reading one of those sometime when you're feeling war-like! Personally, I'm settling down to long years of peace!

Chapter 7

Auf Wiedersehen, Hermann

More than a year would pass before Errol Flynn again set eyes on his itinerant Austrian friend, although the word itinerant barely describes the peregrinations of Hermann Erben. He stayed in Spain after Flynn left and joined the British Red Cross, working on the Loyalist side as a field surgeon—with a trip or two to Berlin to supply the Gestapo with information on German leftists opposing Hitler's Condor Legion. In December of 1937, Erben went to China and spent three months with the Chinese Red Cross. Following that, American citizen Erben paid one of his infrequent visits to the United States, a necessary one in view of the tattered state of his status with the U.S. Immigration and Naturalization Service, a situation made the worse for being on the international listing of drug smugglers.

Erben's initial problem with the naturalization service stemmed from the fact that in 1930, in taking out citizenship, he had claimed five unbroken years of residence in the United States. He had not bothered to declare the long periods spent outside the United States. Such a technicality meant nothing to the cavalier Erben, but it was the root cause of his troubles and resulted in eventual rejection.

If a psychiatric read-out on Flynn might reveal quirks of character, so too would one on Hermann Erben. His personality was one that brought constant negative comment, except from Flynn, and just how effective he was as an espionage agent is open to question. A State Department assessment of him dated March 9, 1940 reads:

> There is a considerable amount of information available on him, and many times the assertion has been made that he is a German agent. While his sympathies are decidedly pro-Nazi, it is questionable whether this person is astute enough to be an agent as his boasting and generally obnoxious demeanor tend to alienate from him persons with whom he comes into contact.

The question of his effectiveness as an agent carries over into his general regard for human life. While Erben doubtless caused men to lose their lives in Spain and in the Second World War, he also worked to save lives as a doctor. He was a more than adequate surgeon and never lacked for work; as a specialist in tropical medicine, he made quite some mark for himself. Perhaps it was this perverse nature that made him appealing to Flynn, whose own humor tended toward the perverse. David Niven said that Flynn "thoroughly enjoyed causing turmoil for himself and his friends." The difference would seem to be that Flynn's charm and sense of fun made him endearing, whereas Erben's personality was of a kind that failed to amuse or endear.

In the spring of 1938, Erben, doubtlessly sensing the need, took a trip to Washington to try to straighten out his affairs. He was interviewed by R.J. Nicholas, who filed this report (File No. 130— Erben, Hermann Friederich) for the Passport Division of the Department of State:

Dr. Erben called at the Department on April 25, 1938, and discussed with me at some length his adventures since his last appearance at the Department. He stated that before leaving this country he made arrangements with the movie actor Errol Flynn to go to Spain with him and that he did not know until his passport was delivered to him in England that we were restricting passport facilities for Spain. He stated that the Consul in England told him to see the Consulate General in Paris regarding the matter as they would have more information at Paris. When he arrived at Paris he made application at the Consulate General for passport facilities for Spain but could not await the Department's report since Flynn was going into Spain at once. He stated that when he received word at Barcelona that his application for the amendment of his passport was disapproved he left Spain immediately and renewed his application in France.

Dr. Erben stated that he had gone into the portion of Spain held by the Loyalist forces for the purpose of spying upon them and particularly upon the Germans serving in the Loyalist army. He stated he had taken about 2,500 pictures while in Spain and that many of these were of Germans who were serving the Government forces. He also obtained the names, home addresses, and names of relatives of such Germans and forwarded the information to the German secret police who investigated in Germany the families of the Loyalist soldiers.

When Dr. Erben made his application for the extension of his passport in Vienna, he had already made arrangements to go to China with the Austrian Medical Organization. After his passport was extended and the same was made not valid for travel to China, he made inquiry and ascertained that the restriction did not apply to Hong Kong. Dr. Erben claims that upon his arrival in Hong Kong he was arrested by the British police and deported to Canton, China, where he got in touch with the American Consul and explained the circumstances of his case and the Consul made arrangements for him to return to Hong Kong from which point he sailed for Kobe, Japan. Upon his arrival in Kobe, Dr. Erben made application to the American Consul there for the amendment of his passport to be valid in China. He claims that he submitted to the Consul documentary evidence of his employment by the Austrian Red Cross and that as a result, the Consul sent the Naval radiogram to the Department. He claims that after the radio was sent, he ascertained that unless he sailed for China at once he could not obtain transportation to Shanghai. He claims that he reported this fact to the Consul and explained to the Consul that he had no funds to pay for his room and board if he remained in Kobe. He alleged that the Consul gave him a letter to the American Consul General in Shanghai explaining the situation and that he had the implied permission of the Consul at Kobe to sail for Shanghai. Dr. Erben left China in the early part of March of this year and arrived at San Diego on March 19. He stated that he worked his way over from China. Dr. Erben requested that his passport be made valid for travel in Spain and China but I told him that the amendments could not be made in the absence of documentary evidence regarding his alleged employment by medical missions. Dr. Erben stated that he desired to go to Spain and enter Madrid with the Rebel forces; then he wants to go to Austria for the purpose of denouncing to the German authorities the Austrian police who caused his arrest a number of years ago and to see they are properly dealt with. While in Germany, he also wants to make arrangements for the return to this country of his two children. Then he desires to go to China to take part in refugee work.

Dr. Erben stated that the Chinese are not interested in medical assistance but that the Japanese will permit assistance to be given to the Chinese in the territory which they hold provided that the assistance is rendered to acceptable aliens. He stated that the Japanese definition of acceptable aliens is "Germans or Americans of German descent." He had with him a number of gruesome pictures of Chinese who had evidently been dead for some time and said that the Japanese permitted him to make such photographs but would not permit ordinary Americans to do so.

Dr. Erben is a very zealous Nazi and showed me the pictures of his two sons in their Nazi uniforms. He was present at the birthday dinner in honor of Hitler held in New York several days ago at which the raid occurred. He was also present in his category as a spy at the meeting held a few days ago in honor of the veterans who returned from Spain.

Dr. Erben thinks that some day the National Socialists will predominate in this country. He is very violent in his dislike for the Jews.

I did not take up Dr. Erben's passport partly because of the absence of evidence that he intentionally violated the restrictions contained therein and partly because he indicated that if he could not obtain a passport he would travel on other documents. I think that a careful check should be made on his activities and that this can be done better by permitting him to travel on an American passport in his own name. I warned Dr. Erben that if he should again violate the conditions of his passport that we would take it up and refuse him further passport facilities even though he was abroad at the time. He promised that he would never again use his passport in violation of the restrictions contained therein and that if he should make an application for the amendment of the passport he would await the Department's decision instead of assuming that the amendment would be authorized. However, I do not think that we can expect that Dr. Erben will keep his promises.

Dr. Erben was familiar with the contents of the Department's confidential cablegram of January 26, 1938, to the Consul General at Shanghai and claims that the consular officer read it to him.

Dr. Erben is now clean-shaven with the exception of a Hitler mustache. He is considerably thinner than when he was last at the Department.

R.J. NICHOLAS

The report by Nicholas points to a bizarre character. Why would any American citizen in 1938, one in danger of not having his passport renewed, boast of being a Nazi? Or freely admit that he attended parties in honor of Hitler in New York? Or that he wanted to bring his sons to America, rabid Nazis that they appeared to be? The two sons—Kurt, born in 1920, and Santos, born in 1922—lived with him in America until 1926 but stayed in Austria afterwards, as did his wife. Erben saw little of his family as he traveled in the 1930s and his wife sued for divorce after the war. At a hearing after the war, he claimed that when he suggested to his sons that they leave Germany and proceed to America they were so incensed that they threatened to denounce him to the authorities for being disloyal to the Nazi cause.

Erben next turned up in Hollywood on September 18, 1938, following a short visit to Vienna and a return to America as the doctor on a Swedish ship that ended up in Los Angeles. Flynn threw a party at the Warner Brothers studio for his guest and Erben was introduced to the likes of Dolores Del Rio, Norma Shearer, Bette Davis, Ramon Novarro and Gary Cooper, with Erben embarrassing Flynn by asking for everyone's autograph. He also took pictures like mad. He photographed Flynn doing a test for *Dodge City* and shot him with Bette Davis doing a scene for *The Sisters*. The next day he took photos of Flynn with Lili Damita, director Edmond Goulding and David Niven. Then came October 21 and goodbye again. Another fleeting visit had come to an end—and there would be only one more.

Things were now getting tougher for Hermann Erben, due to his irresponsible ways with travel documents. While in Los Angeles, his naturalization certificate was lifted by the Immigration and Naturalization Service, who told him they needed to check up on something or other. Whatever it was, they did not return the document to him and without it he could not get employment on any American vessel. Erben paid his passage back to Germany, and in January of 1939, he signed on as surgeon on the German freighter *Wangoni* for a voyage around Africa. In July, he was employed in the same capacity on the *Ussukuma*, which turned out to be the supply ship for the pocket battleship *Admiral Graf Spee*. Erben was off the coast of South America when war broke out on September 3, 1939, and when the *Graf Spee* was crippled by the Royal Navy in Montevideo harbor, Erben was there with his camera to take pictures of the burning, half-sunken hulk. And it was with these pictures that he inveigled his way back into American favor.

Interned by the Argentinians in Buenos Aires, Erben as an American citizen asked for, and received, permission to visit the U.S. Consulate. He presented a hundred photos of the *Graf Spee* incident and volunteered knowledge of German naval affairs. The consul was sufficiently impressed to give Erben the documentation that would clear him from internment and allow him to travel to the United States. He first went overland to Chile, and from Valparaiso, he shipped out as a doctor on board the Grace Lines vessel *Nightingale*, bound for New York. There he dutifully checked in with the FBI and U.S. Navy Intelligence, giving them information about his observations of German shipping movements.

Not allowed to travel outside of the country without a valid passport, Erben became a landlubber and gained a position as a doctor with the CCC (Civilian Conservation Corps), a government job which required citizenship. When the CCC found out that there was some question about the legality of Erben's status they dismissed him. This episode is one which Charles Higham in *The Untold Story* uses as a stick to beat Erben. Higham alludes to the strict security surrounding the CCC camps: "In these, private citizens, mostly young men of close to military age were trained to be ready for soldiering in time of national emergency."

Higham's assessment of the CCC is a little distorted. Set up in 1933, the CCC took unemployed males between the ages of eighteen and twenty-five and put them to work in the national parks and forests. Though the camps were set up by the War Department and though the young men did go through a degree of military regimen, there was nothing military about their activities, which included soil conservation, reforestation methods and the construction of reservoirs. Higham claims that Erben "took numerous photographs of the CCC training methods, installations, guns and other weapons, the layout of the huts and headquarters offices." Aside from the fact that no weaponry was involved in CCC operations, it is questionable what use such photos could be to anyone. What it is, of course, is an attempt to further indict Erben in order to indict Flynn.

When he was dismissed in the summer of 1940, Erben was advised by his lawyer in San Francisco, Chauncey Tramutolo, to come to that city and face an official government hearing and try to solve the problem of his suspended citizenship. Erben was tried by Judge Welsh on September 3 and 4, specifically on the charge that he had obtained citizenship with a declaration that was not completely true, but no judgment was arrived at and Erben was released with the proviso that he remain contactable. After two months, Tramutolo advised Erben to go to Mexico to await the verdict since a negative decision, which now seemed likely, would result in deportation or internment. In Mexico, he would at least be free to go wherever he wished if his American citizenship should be revoked.

Due to his liberal use of Flynn's name every time he was investigated, Flynn himself was visited from time to time by FBI agents wanting to know his views on this trouble-prone friend of his. When Flynn was in Buenos Aires in June of 1940, he was interviewed by ambassador Norman Armour, who handed in this report:

EMBASSY OF THE UNITED STATES OF AMERICA
Buenos Aires, June 21, 1940
DR. HERMANN FRIEDRICH ERBEN
STRICTLY CONFIDENTIAL

The Honorable
The Secretary of State
Washington

Sir:
    With reference to the Consulate General's strictly confidential despatches Nos. 754 and 776 of January 11 and 23, 1940, respec-

tively, transmitting memoranda regarding the activities of Dr. Hermann Friedrich Erben, I have the honor to report that a member of the staff of this Embassy in a conversation with Mr. Errol Flynn, the motion picture actor, verified that Dr. Erben and Mr. Flynn are close friends.

Mr. Flynn stated that he had known Dr. Erben for about ten years and that they had worked together in Spain during the Spanish civil war. He spoke very highly of Erben as a "magnificent physician" who, unfortunately, had a way of getting himself into all sorts of minor difficulties. He stated that the word which most aptly described Dr. Erben was "screwball." He added that Erben had been arrested in India for carrying a pistol and had almost gotten both of them shot in Spain.

He took a very strong stand with respect to Dr. Erben's character and integrity, and stated that Erben would be "the last man in the world to work for the Nazis, as he hated them with all his soul." Mr. Flynn went on to say that he valued Dr. Erben's friendship very highly and that he was a man who certainly could be trusted. However, he stated that the doctor's doing the wrong thing at the wrong time had often created a bad impression on those who did not know him very well. As for being a German agent, he stated that Dr. Erben would probably make the worst agent in the world for any nation, since "they have the finger on him in every port in the world." By this he explained that he meant that in a great many places Dr. Erben had been guilty of some minor infraction of local rules, such as not having the proper papers at the proper time, or saying the wrong thing at the wrong time.

Mr. Flynn added that he understood that Dr. Erben's citizenship had been revoked, and remarked that he had taken the doctor's case up with Mr. Hood of the Federal Bureau of Investigation in Los Angeles and with Mrs. Roosevelt, and that Mrs. Roosevelt had acted in Erben's behalf, but to no avail.

Finally Mr. Flynn stated that he sympathized deeply with Dr. Erben, since he now was a man without a country, and that he felt an injustice had been done the man in believing him to be a German agent, but that no one was to blame but Dr. Erben himself.

As an indication of Dr. Erben's lack of responsibility, it may be mentioned that during his stay in Argentina he made a trip to Montevideo at the time of the *Admiral Graf Spee* incident, despite warnings that his position in Argentina was precarious and he would probably have difficulty in re-entering the country. Upon his return from Montevideo he was imprisoned for want of proper documentation.

Respectfully yours,
NORMAN ARMOUR

Flynn's defense of his friend Erben is admirable albeit rather rash. Anyone who could describe Erben as being a man who could be trusted either did not know the true nature of the man or did not care, and if Flynn knew absolutely nothing about Erben's proclivity for aiding the Nazi cause, then Erben was being as close-mouthed as an agent is supposed to be. In 1980, Erben was interviewed on ABC-TV's "20/20" because of the Higham charges and he said, "If I had been a Nazi spy, I might have been very careful to disguise that until such time as I would have snared him or brainwashed him. Neither snaring nor brainwashing Errol Flynn as a friend was ever attempted by me and never considered."

The most serious charge that Charles Higham brings against Flynn is the aid the actor gave Erben in helping him to escape into Mexico, claiming that for a man who was still a British subject, this was an act of treason against the Crown. In the first place, there was no escape per se and Erben was not, as Higham claims, "a wanted man." Until divested of it, he still had the benefits of American citizenship and he needed no documents to walk across the Mexican border in 1940. It was not yet wartime in America. However, if he had been walking in the other direction it would have been different. And so Higham borders on the preposterous when he claims, "By removing a known Nazi from American soil before justice could take its course, Errol had committed an outright act of treason. As a British subject giving aid and comfort to the enemy, he could have, if caught by British intelligence agents, been extradited and tried in England as a traitor." Higham goes on to say that the famous star

112

might have ended his days at the end of a hangman's rope. The logic of the claim is mind boggling.

Erben arrived in Los Angeles on October 26 and he spent the following two weeks with Flynn. They went sailing on Flynn's ketch *Sirocco*, they went to parties, and on several days, Flynn took him to Warners where he was filming *Footsteps in the Dark*. Erben went to San Francisco on November 10 and it was then that his lawyer advised him that things looked somewhat grim and that it might be best to go to Mexico to await the final verdict on the citizenship hearings. Erben returned to Los Angeles and visited Flynn at Warners on November 13 to say goodbye—and November 13, 1940, was the last time Errol Flynn and Hermann Erben ever saw each other.

The charge that Flynn was responsible for driving Erben into Mexico is false. Warner Brothers records confirm that Flynn was working on *Footsteps in the Dark* at the studio on the fifteenth, the day of the crossing. Erben proceeded by car to Nogales, Arizona, by way of Phoenix and Tucson, arriving in Nogales at 5:15 PM and then walked across the border forty-five minutes later. Whether Erben drove himself or was driven by someone else to Nogales is not clear from his diary entries for those days. He obviously considered it of no importance. If his citizenship had been reaffirmed, he would simply have come back across the border. But that was not to be, and Erben's life was about to change dramatically.

In Mexico City in January 1941, Erben went to see the German Consul, Baron von Wallenberg, who convinced Erben that there was little likelihood of his American citizenship being continued and that it would be better if he worked for the German cause. He offered Erben a salaried position as an agent for the Abwehr which Erben, who freely admitted years later that he loved the whole business of espionage, accepted. He was then sent by ship to Japan. At the time of crossing the Pacific, Erben's citizenship was revoked, something he would not find out about until much later. It is interesting to note that in the declaration of revocation, Erben is

indicted for his false claims and for his record of insufficient report-
ings of his travels, some of it without proper documents, and for his
record as a probable narcotics smuggler. There is no mention in the
declaration of espionage. Indeed, Erben had not been engaged in
such from the outbreak of the war until his crossing into Mexico,
which makes charges of nefarious aid on the part of Flynn pointless.

Abwehr decided that Shanghai would be Erben's base and it was
there that he stayed for the duration of the war. He was told to pose
as an American and to espouse the communist cause, and to report
on British and American movements. Just how effective Erben was
as an agent is difficult to assess. There is no evidence to suggest that
the Germans thought highly of him; indeed, the Abwehr, with by
that time almost no German interest in the Far East, seemingly
dropped Erben in 1943. He was then interned by the Japanese, for
whom he most probably worked as an informant. After the war,
Erben claimed that his interest in becoming an Abwehr agent was
to also aid America as a double agent, but without telling American
intelligence about it. He also claimed that he had saved several
American lives but the evidence points to his having cost more than
he claimed he saved. Erben said that one of the first things he did
upon arriving in Shanghai was to check in with the American
consulate. Apparently he did, but it was not long before the attack
on Pearl Harbor and any aid he might have been willing to give the
American cause evaporated.

Erben's duplicitous nature certainly made him a prime subject
for double agenting, if such he ever was. The Shanghai years put
Erben in a poor and morally shabby light. Like a cockroach he was
intent on surviving, and after the war, he survived by telling all he
knew about German and Japanese wartime activities to American
intelligence.

Charles Higham claims that Flynn was of great service to Erben
as an Abwehr agent by getting an American passport to him in
Shanghai. But why would this have been necessary? The Abwehr
could supply their agents with any documentation they wished.

Forging an American passport was a minor piece of work for German intelligence. Higham also claims that all the wartime correspondence between Flynn and Erben has disappeared, which is not entirely true. Higham maintains that Flynn supplied Erben with military intelligence but if nothing survives then how can the point be made? And what kind of intelligence would Flynn have been able to give? As it turned out, there was almost no German and Japanese espionage or sabotage activity in California during the war years.

Apparently what Errol Flynn most wanted to be during the Second World War was a foreign correspondent, and any understanding of the Flynn mystery—if such a thing there ever was—impinges upon the frustration of that ambition. In my opinion, it is the beginning of the spiritual decline of the man.

The desire for success as a writer never left Flynn, but whatever efforts he made to get a commission as a correspondent met with frustration—until one finally came his way. A letter he wrote Erben in Shanghai on July 18, 1941, gives some indications of what Flynn had in mind. "I still hope I will be able to get over there and join you—some day perhaps toward the end of this year if it is still possible to go there. I am working very hard on trying to get a syndicated newspaper in the East to appoint me their representative in Shanghai, in which case I will be able to join you there. The newspaper syndicate is more than willing but, unfortunately, my nationality comes into the question as I am still, as you know, British." He ends the letter, "It is sad to think that you won't be able to come back to this country soon but I have a feeling that sooner or later when all of this mess is over, you will be able to."

Correspondence between the United States and Shanghai during the war was mostly done through the Red Cross, although Higham claims Flynn used covert diplomatic channels to reach Erben. A telegram dated May 14, 1943, sent through the Red Cross—with the word CENSORED stamped on it—by Erben to Flynn reads: "Dear Pal. Please safeguard the parcel I left with you in November 1940. It contains last letters of my son, killed in action in Russia. Write to me. As ever, your Nurmunger." Nurmunger was Flynn's nickname for Erben. The apparent answer is dated almost two years later, April 9, 1945: "Dear Nurmunger. Your package is safe and I pray heaven you continue to be the same. Always remember your friend is with you. Errol Flynn."

Erben appealed to Flynn for help after the war when he was being investigated for the informing he had done on Britons and Americans during the Shanghai years, although it is doubtful that he told Flynn exactly what the charges against him were. A letter from Flynn dated July 22, 1946, begins: "Hermann, Old Boy, I have just this minute received your letter and hasten to reply. First of all, Robert Ford, my attorney, is going after your case as hard as any Goddam lawyer can be made to go...." The letter then explains that Flynn had not been able to locate Chauncey Tramutolo, and continues with generalities. Ford was Flynn's co-lawyer during the rape trial and one may assume—but again with no evidence one way or the other—that once Ford discovered the nature of the charges against Erben, he chose not to follow through. Be that as it may, Erben continued to name Flynn as a character witness in every statement he made in his defense.

Erben was arrested and jailed by the American Army when Shanghai was entered in August of 1945. He was subjected to hearings over a period of two months, with much bitter comment made about his wartime activities by those he had caused to suffer. However, the charges were not tight enough to indict him and he was let off the hook. By then, it was apparent that Erben could be of considerable value to American intelligence revealing all he knew about the German and Japanese espionage circles in the Far East, and indeed he knew a great deal. At the start of 1946, Erben became an employee of the U.S. Army, serving both as a doctor and as an informant, but a year later, further charges welled up against him and he was once again placed under arrest. The Chinese government bitterly objected to his presence, claiming he had been harmful to them during the war, while at the same time Erben's wartime posing as a communist returned to haunt him. It all resulted in Erben being sent to the U.S. Army Repatriation Center in Ludwigsburg, Germany. He was questioned over the course of several months but never tried. Trying to nail Hermann Erben with specific charges was like trying to swat a fruit fly. By 1948, he was free to go his way—or ways. Erben would continue to be one of the world's most itinerant human beings. His future assignments as a doctor would take him all over the Middle East, the Far East and the South Pacific.

Just how long Flynn and Erben kept up their correspondence is impossible to determine. My guess is that it dwindled away by the end of the 1940s. Flynn was not a man for sustained contact by mail. He did write to Erben when Erben was in the Ludwigsburg detention camp. In a long letter (dated March 1, 1948) to Colonel Amos Moscrip, Jr., who had been his commanding officer during his Army employment in Shanghai, Erben complained about the lack of support he has received from former colleagues, except "The only man who has answered my plight, and sent me a truly wonderful and kind letter, was my old pal Errol Flynn, but he has no official capacity." Presumably Erben at this point would rather have heard from someone less kind but more influential. And I wonder how pleased Flynn would have been had he overheard a remark Erben often made to his wife about Flynn, "Errol was easily bamboozled."

Despite all his indiscretions and his treacherous wartime activities Erben tried very hard to get back to America after the war and resume his citizenship. While the Army may have found him useful, the State Department wanted no part of Hermann Erben. He had played too many middles against too many ends. He was never again allowed to set foot in the United States. In 1954, now with a British wife, he applied for entry into Canada, but after reviewing his background, the Canadians decided he was not someone they wished to have as a citizen.

Erben kept his medical career going for a very long time, right up until 1979 when he returned to his native Vienna, there to spend the remaining six of his eighty-seven years. He lived alone in his eccentricity, a man whose strange and often abrasive personality had left him friendless. The one man he claimed as the true friend of his life, Errol Flynn, had died twenty years before.

By the time Flynn came to write *My Wicked, Wicked Ways*, he had long lost contact with Erben, which presented a problem for the publisher. Erben figured so prominently in the story that they were worried about naming him without his permission. No one seemed to know whether Erben was alive or dead. Flynn and his collaborator, Earl Conrad, were asked to invent a name. They came up with Dr. Gerrit H. Koets. There was no attempt on Flynn's part to cover up his adventures with Erben or not to give him his proper name. The Putnams legal department demanded the change.

After Earl Conrad left Jamaica and went back to New York to work on the manuscript of *My Wicked, Wicked Ways*, he frequently wrote to Flynn to check various points. In response to more information on Erben, Flynn wrote to Conrad from the Hotel Comodoro in Havana, Cuba, on March 24, 1959: "Yes, Erben spoke English with a German accent; although his vocabulary was excellent, there was always a German intonation. Erben was highly articulate, coherent, with a choice vocabulary; slow delivery, knowing what he had to say, or wanted to say, before he said it, and regardless of the slight nuances of delivery, whatever Erben said, you understood it. Even when he spoke horrible Spanish, bastardly Italian, abominable French, you were left with no doubt as to his meaning." That clarity of speech would appear to be one of the few things about Hermann Friedrich Erben that is relatively easy to grasp.

The best assessment of Hermann Erben's character was given by his British-born second wife Joan, whom he met in 1939 but did not marry until 1950. It was an unhappy union and they eventually separated. She viewed Erben as being, like his friend Flynn, an enigma. As a doctor, he was gifted and dedicated. As a man, he was often cold of nature and foolish in his actions and beliefs. In an interview with William Donati, the second Mrs. Erben said, "Politically, I do not believe he thought America would enter the war and that Germany would be the victor. Nonetheless, in characteristic fashion, he wanted to hedge his bet and work for both sides, so that he could claim a reward no matter who won."

Flynn, with that inflated sense of self importance that overtakes people when they become movie stars, behaved stupidly in going to bat for Erben when the Austrian ran into difficulties over his citizenship. Flynn's telegram to Eleanor Roosevelt at the White House, dated March 20, 1940, in which he asked for her help on behalf of Erben, was quite ill-advised, if not downright foolish, especially if he was aware of Erben's admiration for Hitler. The request was denied, and years later, it would surface egregiously in Charles Higham's allegations against Flynn. But what Flynn actually knew about his capricious friend's beliefs and intentions is impossible to determine.

Chapter 8

The *Dive Bomber*
Business

To my mind the most bizarre of Charles Higham's allegations against Errol Flynn are those concerned with the making of the
film *Dive Bomber*, which was largely shot at the United States Naval
Air Station in San Diego, California, in March, April and May of
1941. Flynn is charged with trying to persuade Warner Brothers to
include his own footage of Pearl Harbor and various naval installations, all with a view to aiding Japanese military intelligence. Supposedly, he wanted Warners to film every part of the Naval Air
Station and the carrier *Enterprise* in order to help the upcoming
enemy. Not only does the charge give Flynn credit for what Japanese

spies were actually doing, but it assumes his prior knowledge of the top secret plans to bomb Pearl Harbor half a year later. The charge borders on humor but the unraveling is not without interest. *Dive Bomber* was yet another Warner Brothers warning to the American public of the country's likely future in a world war. Until the spring of 1941, none of the Hollywood studios had ever had any trouble getting cooperation from the Departments of the Army and the Navy in making movies about the services. Regiments and fleets were easily attainable in the hope the film would spark interest in the services. However, the armed forces were now gearing up for war and the Navy at first turned down the Warner request for cooperation in the making of *Dive Bomber* at the San Diego station. It was explained that with the expansion of operations and the increased numbers of men and planes, filming might get in the way. Jack Warner was not about to be deterred, so he sent one of his top executives, Colonel William Guthrie, a man of military diplomacy, to Washington to discuss the matter with Frank Knox, the Secretary of the Navy. Permission was granted and filming began on March 20, 1941, with Flynn and the other principal actors arriving two weeks later. During the month or so that Flynn was working on the production, he, Fred MacMurray and Ralph Bellamy were comfortably quartered in the famed Hotel del Coronado, less than a mile from the main gates of the North Island naval air station. They were at all times transported by naval cars and drivers and under surveillance continuously.

Before filming began, the script, by naval air veteran Frank Wead in collaboration with Robert Buckner, was carefully checked by the Navy, and since civilians cannot give orders to military personnel while on duty at a base, director Michael Curtiz was assigned two officers, Lieut. Commander Seth Warner and Lieut. Commander Charles Brown, through whom Curtiz had to relay all his wishes for naval movement. Other officers were assigned for liaison duty with Warner Brothers executives and technicians. The Higham charges that Curtiz went around the base screaming orders at sailors, like

"Hey, you bums, get back in line!" or yelling at an admiral, "Hey, you gold braid bum, get back there! Get out of the shot!" are, therefore, patently absurd.

Michael Curtiz, the top Warner director for some thirty years, was a hard-driving, often arrogant taskmaster, who offended actors with his lack of concern for their comfort. Flynn had grown to hate him and after *Dive Bomber* refused to ever work with him again, despite the fact that many of Flynn's classic films, like *Captain Blood, Robin Hood* and *The Sea Hawk,* had been achieved under Curtiz's tough command.

Ralph Bellamy recalls, "Curtiz had to be on his best behavior on that picture. He was used to calling the shots, but this time the Navy was doing the ordering. Many of the aviation sequences had to be done in one take because they [the Navy] were not about to do another. But even though Curtiz couldn't give any direct orders to the sailors, he was always grabbing officers by their sleeves as they walked by and saying things like 'My good man, do you think you could go over there and do this for me,' or 'Excuse me, my good fellow, would you mind walking over there for me.' No, he didn't call anybody a bum. Jack Warner would have yanked him out of there by the seat of his pants if he had done so."

Dive Bomber was released in August of that year and met with respectable reviews. At a cost of $1.7 million, it was by far the most expensive military film yet made by Hollywood, and at two hours and thirteen minutes, the longest. Superbly filmed in Technicolor, it was a tribute to the doctors and the medical researchers of naval aviation. The plot in brief: Lt. Douglas Lee (Flynn) graduates from the Naval Flight Surgeon School in San Diego and is assigned to Lt. Commander Dr. Lance Rogers (Bellamy). The two of them work toward a solution for the problem of pilot blackout, embolism and fatigue while performing in high altitudes, in particular the problems faced in dive bombing. Flight Commander Joe Blake (Mac-Murray) thinks little of the doctors, especially the blithe and breezy Lee, but after one of his friends dies from pilot fatigue, he agrees to cooperate and becomes convinced of the importance of the work. He dies while testing a new pressurized flying suit, but not before he is able to write a note which gives Rogers and Lee the clue to perfecting the suit, which makes it possible for the doctors to solve the problem of blackout while diving.

The idea that Errol Flynn would have any say in the filming of *Dive Bomber* is ridiculous. He may have been a top box office star but he was still a Warner Brothers employee, working for bosses who seldom took suggestions from actors. Flynn's fellow contractees, Bette Davis and James Cagney, often objected to projects and went on suspension rather than film them. Flynn never did. He may have complained, but his philosophy was always "take the money and run—and have fun spending it."

The associate producer for the film was Robert Lord, who had worked in that capacity on several Flynn films. Lord had been with Warners since 1926 as a writer and turned producer in 1938 for Flynn's *The Dawn Patrol*, working under the studio's head of production Hal. B. Wallis. The term *associate producer* at that time signified one who actually supervised the production under the executive direction of Wallis. But it is because of Robert Lord that Flynn comes under suspicion during the making of this film. Charles Higham claims that Lord said to him:

> I do not want this statement published until after I'm dead. In our advance prints of the picture, before it was released, we used most of Errol's land and air shots of Pearl Harbor at his suggestion in a special, semi-documentary presentation of America's power in the Pacific.
>
> An advance print was sent to our representatives in Japan in the normal course of events in the late summer of 1941. Needless to say, it was examined with great interest by the Japanese Chiefs of Staff. It proved to be most valuable to them in their plans for an attack on Pearl Harbor.
>
> It's also shocking to think in retrospect that again at Errol's suggestions, we showed every detail of the San Diego Naval Base and

the entire structure of the *Enterprise*. I believe that the Japanese kept the film under study for years in case of a possible assault on California.

If what Robert Lord told Charles Higham is true, it would make Lord himself suspect. Every line of the script and every camera shot had to be approved by the Navy, and once the film was assembled, it was taken to Washington and edited under naval supervision. A number of shots were excised. Also, there is no record in the Warner Brothers archives of any semi-documentary film involving *Dive Bomber*. It is true Flynn was on vacation in Hawaii just before working on the film and it is also true that he took with him his 16mm camera. But could he have taken any shots of naval installations undetected? And would Warners have used such material by an amateur photographer? On the other hand, it is likely that Flynn would try to sell footage to Warners simply for money. He was always dunning the studio and he delighted in marking up every cost to them that he could get away with.

Robert Lord died in April of 1976 at the age of seventy-five. Higham apparently interviewed him in Los Angeles in 1970, quite a while before starting to write the Flynn book in 1978. In the expanded softback version of *The Untold Story*, Higham further quotes Lord as saying, "I should have been suspicious of Flynn's constant insistence that we shoot on location on the USS *Enterprise* and in San Diego Naval Base." Again, how could the actor have had the least say in the choice of locations specified in the Navy-approved script?

The Higham-Lord statement is also at variance with a letter Lord wrote on July 8, 1941, to W.J. McCord, the head of the Warners editing department. (The Letter is in the Warner Archives at the University of Southern California.) In it, Lord points out that the Warner contract with the Navy specifies editing approval, prior to the footage previously being shown anywhere, and that it will be necessary for Lord and McCord to fly to Washington for an editing conference. He adds, "This is especially true now since the United

States is in a state of national emergency and the Navy is triply careful..."

Ralph Bellamy agrees with the Higham version of the filming of *Dive Bomber* only in regard to describing the rigors of filming on the aircraft carrier *Enterprise*. "We put to sea with them for a week. We didn't need all that time but it was the only way we could get the shots we needed. It was a war maneuver and the admiral in charge and the captain of the carrier really didn't want us along. We were in the way and they really let us know it. The first night out, they kept up battle practice and none of us got any sleep. I'd worked with Mike Curtiz before, but this was the first time I'd ever seen him humbled. He was used to being a dictator, but not on this trip. Mike probably thought he was pretty tough until he came up against that navy brass. All through the picture, he would get notification as to when and where planes were taking off, and if he couldn't get there on time, too bad. I remember one day on the *Enterprise* he was shooting planes taking off, and smoke from the carrier stack was coming in the direction of his shot. He went up to one of the officers and said, 'Please, sir. Could you get the smoke to go in the other direction?'"

How did Flynn behave? "Beautifully. In fact it would have been tougher for us without him. Errol was a very affable and amusing kind of fellow. He had this upper-crust British manner about him and by the end of the trip he had everybody eating out of his hand—except the admiral and the captain. I enjoyed being with him. We played tennis together, although I could never beat him, and neither could anybody else. While we were staying at the hotel, he had his boat, the *Sirocco*, brought down from Newport and it was moored at the Coronado Yacht Basin. We used to go out on the weekends and it was a lot of fun."

What about Flynn as an actor? "Well, he was very good at what he did. He had an air of bravado about him and it was just right for these action pictures. The critics have this lame-brained idea that you don't have to be very talented to play a swashbuckler. That's nonsense. I wouldn't have been any good playing Robin Hood or a pirate captain and I don't know many actors who can bring that kind of thing off with any style or conviction. Flynn could, although I don't think he himself realized how good he was at it. He didn't seem to have much confidence as an actor and maybe because of that he sort of made light of the whole thing."

Did Flynn voice any political sentiment during the making of *Dive Bomber?* "Not a word. I doubt whether a political thought ever crossed his mind. I know he liked Roosevelt. He showed me an autographed photo from FDR, but it was more like a movie fan showing a picture of his favorite star. If Errol had any political beliefs, he certainly kept that to himself. I've heard about him supposedly having been an enemy agent. I don't see how. If he was working for the other side, then the way he covered it up would make him the greatest actor I have ever come across in all my many years in the theater and the movies."

Flynn is also fondly remembered from the *Dive Bomber* filming by Alexis Smith and Craig Stevens, both of whom had small roles and for whom it was the start of a romance that led to marriage. Says Stevens, "Errol was very nice to both of us. I was just starting out as an actor and he was encouraging. Shortly after that, I went into the service for a couple of years. When I came out, Alexis and I got married, June of '44, and Errol came to the wedding. He came up to me at the reception and said, as if he were her father, 'Look Sport, if you don't do right by this girl you're going to have to answer to me.'"

Alexis Smith went on to star with Flynn in *Gentleman Jim* (1942), *San Antonio* (1945) and *Montana* (1950). She was nineteen at the time of working with him in *Dive Bomber*. "He was a movie idol of my teens and when I was playing opposite him, I was intimidated. I came to like him genuinely. Yes, he was full of tricks and flip and always had an entourage of girls. But he could charm anyone, man or woman, and his charm continued to the end. I'll never forget a day he came on the set of *Montana* loaded and continued to drink.

His eyes were bloodshot and they needed close-ups. So they called a doctor and everyone waited. The doctor came out of Flynn's dressing room about half an hour later and *he* wasn't walking straight. So we were all sent home. But Flynn was also intelligent, and he had wit. It's a shame he cared more for the bottle and for fun and games than he did for work."

The idea that Errol Flynn would have done anything to help the Japanese strikes me as more of a strained theory than that he would have aided the Germans. His generation of Australians had little regard for "the Yellow Race." He and his family were typical White Anglo-Saxon Protestants of the Old Colonial School. Some indication of his attitude toward Orientals can be found in a letter Flynn wrote to his father from Kavieng on August 17, 1928: "Do you know the other day I was fined ten pounds for hitting a Chinaman who called me by my surname without Mr. or Master before it. The Chinamen here are coolies or were, and they are little better than Kanakas. They are becoming impossibly cheeky and what's more they are getting away with it—and why? Because the League of Nations recognises these coolies to be of equal status with the white man."

With third wife Patrice Wymore on board the *Zaca* in the Mediterranean in 1953. The yacht was their main home for much of the early Fifties.

With Patrice and their daughter Arnella, born in Rome in 1954. Two years later they came to Hollywood, where Flynn appeared in *Istanbul*, made entirely on the backlot at Universal.

In 1957, the sagging Flynn career picked up with his boisterous and charming portrayal of Mike Campbell in *The Sun Also Rises*. In one of its most amusing scenes Flynn and Eddie Albert challenge the bulls in Pamplona. (Rick Dodd Collection)

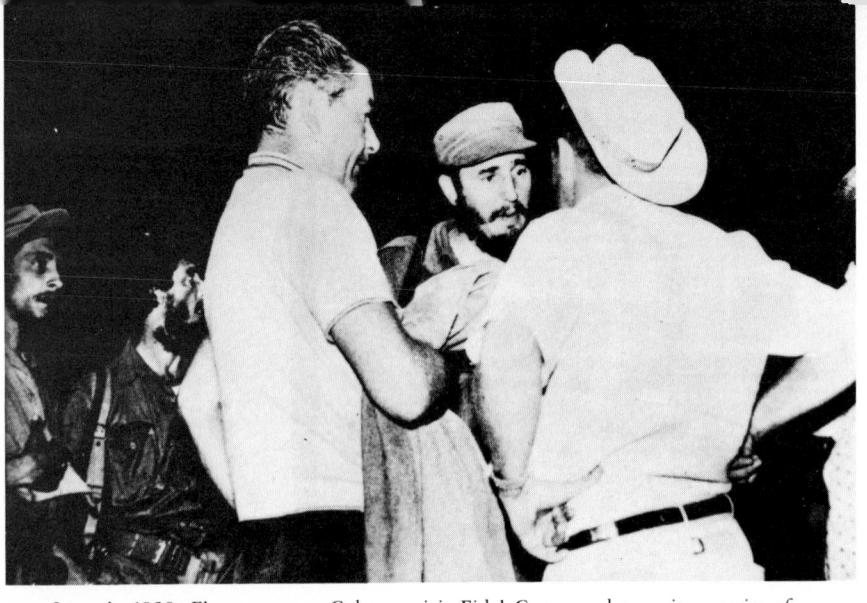

In early 1959, Flynn went to Cuba to visit Fidel Castro and to write a series of articles on the Cuban Revolution for the *New York Journal-American*. It was his last fling at being a writer, in this case the dying ember of the old dream about being a war correspondent. (Rick Dodd Collection)

In October of 1958, writer Earl Conrad joined Flynn in Port Antonio, Jamaica, to put together the celebrated *My Wicked, Wicked Ways*. Most of it was done at the Titchfield Hotel, then owned by Flynn, with time off now and then to sit around the pool. (Earl Conrad Collection)

In September 1959, Flynn asked Nora and their daughters Deirdre and Rory to meet him at Los Angeles Airport, to discuss provisions in his revised will that would provide for them. Such a revision never came to be. Says Nora, "I had to wear glasses because I was crying, he looked so ill. He said his doctors had told him he had a year to live. It turned out to be not much more than a month."

In the first week of October, Flynn appeared on *The Red Skelton Show*, playing a gentleman hobo in a sketch with Skelton, here in rehearsal. With Flynn is his constant companion for the last year and a half, seventeen-year-old Beverly Aadland.

Flynn in his fling on *The Red Skelton Show*, his final professional appearance.

In Vancouver, B.C. on October 12th, 1959, two days before his death. This is possibly the last photo ever taken of him.

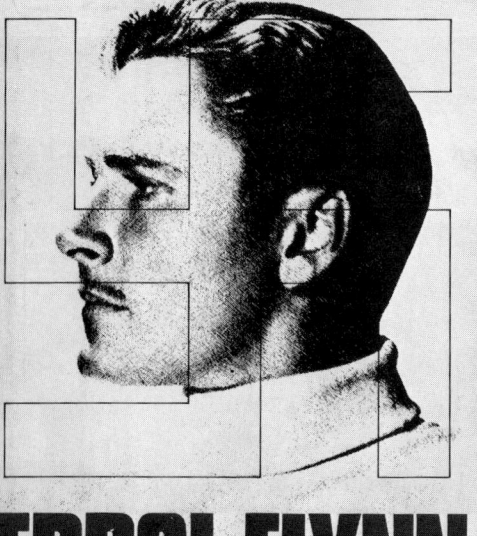

The cover of Charles Higham's 1979 book raised eyebrows. Why the swastika? When the book came out in a softback version a year later the swastika was even more accentuated, along with "shocking new documentary evidence never before published."

The cover of the British version of the Higham book would suggest it to be the story of a major Nazi, perhaps one ranking with the likes of Goebbels or Ribbentrop.

This impression by Trudy McVicker of Flynn in his final years suggests some of the regret he may have felt, despite his bravura front. He writes, "Flynn was Jekyll and Hyde and everything in between. He was a fascinating and tragic man torn apart by his own complexity, gifted but sadly insecure and with no strong core to keep him balanced. For Flynn the struggle for self-realization was sabotaged by his beauty and his charm and his charisma. Those qualities opened all doors for him—far too easily, far beyond his wildest dreams. And so, inside he remained unfinished and incomplete."

Chapter 9

The Would-Be Spy

Those who defend Errol Flynn against alleged involvement in espionage on the grounds that he was too much of a playboy, too lighthearted and unreliable to be a spy are only partly right. As David Niven once said about him, "Errol was a many-sided creature." Some of those sides tended to be introverted and somewhat dark. Although charming and amusing socially, Flynn in private read serious literature and mused on the mystery of humankind. From all I have learned of this complex man, I can well imagine him being intrigued with the idea of espionage, if for no other reason than to write about it.

Flynn was, in fact, involved in a little espionage—but not for the Germans. After the outbreak of war in 1939, the whole British colony in Hollywood was expected to support the cause. A few members of that once well-populated and very British corner of the Empire went back to England to join the services but most were too old and contented themselves with waving the Union Jack and supporting British War Relief, along with rallying behind such causes as Bundles for Britain. On a more vital and less conspicuous level, the Hollywood Britons were asked to help combat American neutrality. Just as it was obvious that Britain alone could not have emerged victorious in the First World War, it was now even more obvious that without American support the British stood little chance against the power of Nazi Germany.

Hollywood was vital to the British cause in the first two years of the war, and the pro-British, anti-Nazi stand of the studios had a substantial effect on American consciousness. Most of the studios were then owned and managed by Jews, who had every reason to look with trepidation upon Hitler and his plans for the world. Warner Brothers took the lead in this anxiety. They began making anti-Nazi films even before the outbreak of the war. Their *Confessions of a Nazi Spy*, released in May of 1939, was the first movie to deal with the German underground in America. Once the Germans invaded Poland, the film studios of Hollywood virtually went to war.

Just how well the British Empire would have done without the enthusiastic support of Franklin Delano Roosevelt hardly needs any dwelling upon in these pages. More to the point is the support from Hollywood, which included British producers like Herbert Wilcox making *Nurse Edith Cavell*, starring his wife Anna Neagle and made at RKO, and Alexander Korda turning out *That Hamilton Woman*, with Vivien Leigh as Emma Hamilton and Laurence Olivier as Horatio Lord Nelson, an inspiring epic made in the small General Services Studios on Melrose Avenue, opposite Paramount. Released in England to enormous success with the better title of *Lady Hamilton*, it was said to be Winston Churchill's favorite film. It is not hard to understand his pleasure; the film could hardly have waved the flag more vigorously had it been filmed on the Thames with the ghost of Nelson giving directions.

The parallels between Nelson's heroic stand against Napoleon's fleet at Trafalgar and Churchill's defiance of Hitler's possible invasion of England were clear enough in *That Hamilton Woman*, just as they were in Flynn's classic swashbuckler, *The Sea Hawk*, released by Warners in July of 1940 and for which they supplied a different ending for the British release. In this rousing picture, Flynn plays a Sir Francis Drake-like privateer who helps save Elizabethan England from the ambitions of Spain to conquer the world. The American version ends with Flynn being knighted by the Queen, but in the extended British version, she goes on to say, " . . . when the ruthless ambitions of a man threaten to engulf the world it becomes the solemn obligations of free men, wherever they may be, to affirm that the earth belongs not to any one man, but to all men . . ." No one could accuse Jack L. Warner and his brothers of not doing their bit.

Errol Flynn was not, in my opinion, a man of any patriotic fervor and I doubt if his toes tapped to any national anthem. He showed no interest in returning to either England or Australia when war was declared, although he did volunteer to do some pep-talk broadcasts for the Australians. He had by then registered for American citizenship, for which he received his final papers on August 14, 1942. In a letter to the *Los Angeles Times*, in rebuttal to one of my own defending Flynn, Charles Higham claimed that the actor had secured his citizenship falsely with the aid of high ranking Immigration and Naturalization Service officers who were Nazis. Since by that time Flynn had lived in the United States continuously for seven and a half years, he was more than legally qualified. Thirty-two years of age when America joined the war, Flynn was given a U.S. Army medical examination in February of 1942 and found to be 4-F, which caused some critics to be doubtful because Flynn looked so splendidly fit. The tuberculosis, the recurrent malaria and the irregular heart beat were not visible. Any fighting Flynn would do in the Second World War would have to be done in front of cameras.

Flynn made only five films that dealt with that war. The first was the absurd adventure romp *Desperate Journey* (1942), in which he is an RAF bomber pilot, shot down over Germany, fighting his way back to England, causing havoc for the Nazis all the way. This film is oddly described by Higham in *The Untold Story* as being about an Australian army in Europe. In the much better *Edge of Darkness* (1943), Flynn is the leader of a Norwegian underground uprising against the occupation; in the mediocre *Northern Pursuit* (1944), he is a Canadian mountie thwarting a team of Nazi saboteurs; and in *Uncertain Glory* (1944), Flynn appears as a French criminal who turns noble and sacrifices himself for the underground cause. His best war film was *Objective, Burma!* (1945), in which he portrayed an American army captain leading a mission behind Japanese lines. Although he was lampooned by the critics as a man winning the war single-handedly on the screen, Flynn made fewer war films than most actors, certainly fewer than John Wayne.

The only wartime film in which Flynn seemingly enjoyed himself was *Thank Your Lucky Stars* (1943), in which in a song-and-dance cameo he appears as a cheeky cockney sailor in a London pub. He brags of his imaginary exploits shooting down the Luftwaffe over London, wiping out German regiments in North Africa and sinking Japanese ships in the Pacific. The other patrons celebrate him in chorus, "Hurray, he's won the war," to which Flynn responds, "Yes, and I won the one before." An amusing piece of material and a good performance, it pointed toward Flynn as a better entertainer than the typecasting of hero forced upon him by Warner Brothers. But the business of Hollywood is business and Flynn was a box office winner of wars.

The involvement of movie stars in covert wartime espionage has been much exaggerated. The last time I saw David Niven was in April of 1981 when we worked together on the television special *The American Film Institute Salute to Fred Astaire,* for which he was the host. We talked about Flynn in regard to the Higham charges.

Niven had been one of the few major names to speak up for Flynn—Hollywood is a cautious and not very brave community—and he had written a letter to the London *Times* expressing his disgust. Since he had played the legendary espionage leader, Sir William Stevenson, in the telefilm, *A Man Called Intrepid*, I asked him if there was any truth to the rumor that he had actually worked for Stephenson. He said emphatically that he had not and that "all this talk about movie stars being used as spies is just a lot of bloody nonsense. Most actors I wouldn't rely upon as capable guides to the bathroom." He went on to say that of all the stars named as having done espionage work, the only two he knew for certain were Noel Coward and Leslie Howard. How about Flynn as a German spy? "Ludicrous, absolutely bloody ludicrous. What would he spy on? The color of Jack Warner's underpants?" How about Flynn having done some work for British Intelligence? "I really don't know. I've heard that and it's possible he might have done something. All the Brits in Hollywood were asked to speak well of the old country and to keep their eyes and ears open. But you're not going to be able to prove anything because Stephenson won't say a damn thing and the fellows in Whitehall aren't going to give you any help one way or the other."

Niven was correct in assessing the British Ministry of Defence in regard to commenting on official documents pertaining to wartime espionage. However, persistence sometimes pays off, even with the British. In collecting material for his own refutation of the Higham charges, William Donati received this reply:

> We see no reason to question the reported statement of his friend and fellow actor David Niven that the suggestion that Errol Flynn was a spy as a "lot of nonsense."

> Lt. Colonel D.A. Betley, MBE,
> RRF
> Ministry of Defence
> Whitehall, London.
> May 6, 1981.

My friend and researcher, Trudy McVicker, was also able to elicit a small response from Sir William Stephenson, much to the surprise of Niven and others. In a shaky handwritten note from his home in Bermuda he wrote in 1980:

> I am unaware of any connections Flynn had with any Nazi department and doubtless the FBI would have had knowledge of it if he had. Appears nonsensical on face of it.

A hint of Flynn's possible involvement on behalf of British Intelligence welled up in the wake of the Higham book when reporter, Ian Ball, of the London *Daily Telegraph*, wrote, "...a friend of Sir William, who talked with him after the Flynn disclosures were made last month, told me yesterday that Sir William had said flatly that 'Errol Flynn was not a German spy.'" Ball also offered the opinion, "Flynn was, in fact, dabbling in intelligence work, but doing so as part of Sir William's army of amateur spies..." Whether he realized it or not, Ian Ball had hit on the dilemma of Flynn as an espionage agent with his use of the word *dabbling*. The term *dabbler*, unfortunately, fits Flynn all too well.

Errol Flynn spent six weeks in the summer of 1940 making a so-called "goodwill" tour of Central and South America, visiting twenty-one countries. The tour seemed to have no official sanction, but the fact that he was met and entertained by British diplomats in the major cities points to the tour as being on behalf of the British government, who had good reason to worry about Latin America. The Nazi presence in that part of the world was strong and obvious, which is a major reason for it becoming a Nazi haven after the war. Hitler intended to dominate South America and by doing so intimidate the United States into cooperation, if not actual conquest.

Flynn's trip was motivated by a need to help the British government stem the growing Nazi tide of infiltration in Latin America, and Flynn rose to the occasion as if playing the lead in one of his swashbuckling pictures. When he got back to Los Angeles he held a press conference and said, "The United States is still in a dream and has not awakened to the grave dangers small organized minorities are precipitating. I made it my business to investigate fifth column activities. The danger to America is very near."

In Santiago, Chile, Flynn was the guest of British Ambassador Sir Charles Bentinck, with whom he attended a benefit banquet for the British Red Cross. In Rio de Janeiro, he did broadcasts and then sent copies of the scripts to his one political idol, Franklin Delano Roosevelt, who replied with gratitude and told him to keep up the good work. The front page of the June 25, 1940, edition of the Buenos Aires newspaper *Defensa* carried a handwritten note from Flynn reading, "To the *Defensa*—with every hope for your success, which from your anti-Nazi policy should be of great importance to every lover of liberty."

Upon his return, Flynn told the Los Angeles *Examiner*, "The ordinary people of Latin America are generally friendly to us but higher political and business circles show definitely growing German infiltration. Nazi representatives and sympathizers are making no secret of their intentions to control South American markets and they are working industriously to weaken economic ties between the Latin American countries and the United States."

Flynn also told a reporter that he flew to Mexico City from Santiago, Chile, with a German diplomat who was on his way to the Pan American economic conference being held in Havana, Cuba. "It is typical of the thorough, painstaking way Germany is building up its influence."

Flynn's comments were printed and forgotten. They were not the kind of things people wanted to hear from the handsome, playboy movie star. Throughout Latin America, he had been mobbed by young ladies and he showed every evidence of having had a good time. This was the kind of copy expected of him. A reporter who took him more seriously was William A. Ulman, Jr., a free-lancer Flynn had known soon after his arrival in Hollywood. Ulman thought a story on Flynn's political observations would be easy to place but soon found it was not. The only magazine interested was *Photoplay*, and they asked that it be toned down. What emerged was a piece called "The Man Who Found a Country" (December 1940), the thrust being that footloose Flynn, a man of no fixed abode, was showing the signs of becoming a concerned citizen. Flynn told Ulman, "You see, when I went down to Central and South America, I did not go down there on a binge, despite what you may think." He explained that he wanted to do some good, something "to offset the stupendous amount of damage the totalitarian states are trying to do to us—the United States—with our nearest and dearest neighbors. They—Germany and Italy—are getting ready to fight *us*—not just the British Empire—and they want to fight us in our own back yard—South America. I know! I was there. I saw the preparations, the 'tourists,' the Fifth Columnists, the huge radio programs, the saboteurs. I fought them every way I could. That's why I went."

Obviously carried away by excitement in this telling of his trip, Flynn then pulled from his pocket a sheet of folded newspaper and said, "And furthermore, I've got a diploma!" He proudly showed it to Ulman. "This is it! It's the front page of the *Giornal d'Italia*—that Virgino Gayda's paper, mouthpiece for old Musso himself. They gave me quite a writeup. According to Virgie, himself, I'm the tops! The deadliest, dirtiest, conniving son of a macaw that that unspeakably cunning British Propaganda Ministry has ever sent out."

It is a pity Ulman printed this part of his interview with Flynn because, in my view, this is what brought Errol Flynn's work as a British agent to a swift and sudden close. He had done the one thing an agent must never do—he had called attention not only to what he was doing but he had named the people for whom he had done it. He was never again asked by the British government to do anything, just as they have never admitted he ever did anything for them anyway. And it is the probable reason the American government never used him either, much as Flynn tried to get in on wartime work. The best evidence of his attempts to persuade Washington to use him lies in a letter he wrote to Colonel William J. Donovan, who was put in command of Central Intelligence once America was in the war. It was the agency that Donovan would develop into the Office of Strategic Services, the fabled OSS, which in time would evolve into the CIA.

On February 4, 1942, Donovan wrote to President Roosevelt:

The following letter from Errol Flynn, Hollywood movie star, comes to me in this way. Wallace Deuel, who is in our Foreign Information Service, I loaned to Henry Morganthau to help make a movie. Deuel is in Hollywood and there met Flynn and delivered the message concerning which I talked to you at dinner. If you think there is any need for me to discuss the matter with him, I will have him come over.

Here is the Flynn letter in its entirety:

Many thanks for your message in the wire you sent Mr. Deuel. It has encouraged me to write directly, although I can't help recalling some advice once given me that one should never try to write about any matter of importance if you can't get it on one page of paper. But for the fact that I am working on a picture, I would have flown to Washington, since I firmly believe I have a sound enough idea to warrant taking up some of your time. However, if, as I now outline it briefly, you feel it is of sufficient interest, I am pretty sure I could arrange to fly East in a few weeks to discuss it with you in more detail. Meanwhile, I hope you'll bear in mind that there are many more facts to the scheme than can possibly be put on paper.

My father, Professor T. Thomson Flynn, is Dean of the Faculty of Science at Queen's University, Belfast; and since he has made a life-long practice of disassociating himself with all forms of politics, the result is that he is persona grata and, I might add, pretty highly regarded in Eire also.

The Faculty of Trinity College, Dublin, has invited him to lecture there many times, so I think it will be apparent to you that when a Northern Irish professor is extended invitations of this sort he must not only be in good standing with intellectual circles but official as well—this is important to remember.

And if before the war he was a prominent figure in Northern Ireland I think it can safely be said that he is now also a beloved one, since for these two past years he has been the head of the A.R.P. (Air Raid Precautions) for the entire North, and is generally credited with having secured for the unfortunates there a greater measure of war relief from England than they would otherwise have received.

Now quite apart from my father's situation there, perhaps you know that the Irish, both North and South, are great movie goers. When last there it was a constant source of astonishment to me that while Bridget O'Toole had only the foggiest notion whether the Panama Canal divides America or Africa, she did know without a shadow of a doubt that Clark Gable cherishes a marked antipathy for striped underwear and that Hedy Lamarr wears a false bust. In short she shows the same keen interest in Hollywood personalities that a wife displays going through a husband's pockets. It was most apparent that if the somewhat stolid Northern Irish could get excited about something, that something was Hollywood, and in the South I was a little shocked to discover that the Irish, whom I had always regarded as a little above the average in intelligence, had their share of the slightly hysterical movie fan.

Now in view both of this well-disposed attitude toward me personally as a Hollywood figure plus my father's position there and his many invaluable connections in both North and South, it seems to me that if Uncle Sam were to put me in an American Army uniform and send me over there I could be of value to your department. Without knowing the Government attitude, one presumes America needs the Irish bases in the South, that we must eventually try by every means to secure the use of them. I could work as well, perhaps better, than most to this end, and while the Eire government might possibly see in me an instrument of American propaganda, I feel I could eventually manage to achieve something, particularly toward helping mold the public's opinion to a more favorable view of the Irish base question.

In one other respect I am convinced I could be of considerable use;

that is, the excellent opportunities which seem to come, almost without effort on my part, to a man in my peculiar position in life, to acquire a certain sort of intimate information that would be of use to your department. I have found this to be a fact in the past during my travels in foreign countries; in particular South America a couple of years ago, advance information came to my knowledge often which, to my surprise, was subsequently confirmed by later events. One example of this was that I happened to learn of the forthcoming movements of Arthur Dietrich, the head figure of the Nazi consular-espionage ring and at that time resident in Mexico, a full week *before* he made them. I passed the information on to General Brett and General Dargue who happened to be flying on Army business through Guatemala and I know they both wondered how the devil I, a Hollywood actor, should get hold of this sort of dope. But without going into the exact way it works, it is precisely because one is that that disarms suspicion. In Ireland the opportunities would be, I know, legion. In other words, if I were to go there openly, as a Hollywood figure in an American Army uniform, I would be far less suspected of gathering information than the usual sort of agent. A Hollywood movie star, behaving innocuously, tritely like a Hollywood movie star, would not, I am sure, excite suspicion of the above kind of activity.

There are, of course, so many more angles to this general scheme as to make it impossible to go into them here. And besides this, I am quite sure, Colonel, that you yourself, from your knowledge of Government needs in this matter, will know of many others. But I am most strongly convinced that, by representing a certain large section of public good will in Ireland, I can be of substantial use to you over there.

May I hope to hear from you soon?

Very sincerely,
ERROL FLYNN

There is no documented response to President Roosevelt's reaction to the Flynn proposal but one may assume he smiled and told Donovan to politely decline. The idea of a uniformed Flynn traipsing around Ireland trying to pick up information probably amused the President. Picking up girls would be more like the Flynn image. However, Flynn was not about to give up, and while his efforts to wangle his way into espionage failed, he did finally get what he wanted in the way of a commission as a foreign correspondent. He became friendly with Wallace Deuel, whose job under Donovan gave him access to all the news services and who went to bat for Flynn. One day, Deuel received this happy letter, dated September 30, 1942:

Dear Wally:

Hope you won't think too badly of me for not dropping you a line before this in answer to the one you wrote me in August.

Will you thank Mary for her message to me when I was sick—and thank you, old boy. The prospect of spending months in bed— alone—was a little too much and I rapidly overcame my indisposition by steady and judicious use of alcohol. I have some great news, finally got the spot I wanted, leaving pretty soon, war correspondent for I.N.S. Don't know where I'm heading for yet but I think it will be either France or Australia.

Old Mr. Hearst—fantastic old man—bent a cold eye on me before I was even half-way through my sales talk and squeaked "I think it's a very good idea. When do you want to leave?"

If and when I come through New York I will certainly look you up, Wally, and get some advice from you as to the personal habits, etc., of correspondents. I know you can give me a lot of help and don't think you'll mind doing so.

All the very best to you both,

ERROL FLYNN

Flynn's ecstasy was short-lived. The sky was about to drop on him. A few days after he wrote this letter, two detectives from the Los Angeles Police Department appeared on his doorstep and served him with a warrant on charges of statutory rape. A short time later,

Flynn was formally arrested, taken downtown and placed in a cell for several hours until his lawyers could arrange bailed release.

Errol Flynn found himself plastered all over the newspapers and the butt of jokes by all the comedians. "Hey, did you hear what happened to Errol Flynn? He drowned in Veronica Lake!" "In like Flynn" became a national cry and the coverage of his trial all through January of 1943 assumed *divertissement* proportions amid the grim war news. He laughed about it all but from then on the image of Flynn as roisterer was firmly fixed.

Despite the acquittal and the increased fame, Flynn probably never rid from his inner ear the voice of Prosecutor Cochran describing him at length as a sex criminal of the lowest order and a man who should be jailed. The masterly Jerry Giesler cleared Flynn of all the charges brought by the two girls and their counsels but what those charges did to him on a personal level can only be imagined. What they did to his chances of being taken seriously as a war correspondent or anything on an official level was all too obvious.

Chapter 10

Evidence... and the Lack Thereof

In my opinion, Charles Higham's *Errol Flynn: The Untold Story* is the most extraordinary book of its kind ever written. I know of no other in which an entertainment celebrity has been vilified on such an extravagent scale, and certainly none in which a major Hollywood figure has been accused of being an enemy agent in wartime and a traitor to his own people. If the charges had been true, the book would have been a sensational exposé of a man operating behind a magnificently false facade, and the basis for a spectacular and juicy movie. Hollywood has little pity. For the sake of a good story it will eat its own. But for that to have happened, the charges against Flynn would have had to be beyond refutation, instead of tissues of supposition and implication.

Charles Higham has never wavered in his charges. In the spring of 1989, while touring to publicize *Cary Grant: The Lonely Heart* written in collaboration with Roy Mosely and published by Harcourt Brace Jovanovich, he appeared on ABC's *Good Morning, America*. Host Charles Gibson alluded to Higham's claim that Grant knew about Flynn's treason, and Higham affirmed that it was an irony that a man who performed so heroically on the screen was actually working for the other side. The host chose not to challenge the viewpoint on this widely watched network broadcast. Unfortunately time is of the essence on morning talk shows. Authors plugging books are good for about two minutes.

When *The Untold Story* first appeared in early 1980 it caused all the huffing and puffing its author and publisher could have ever hoped for, some of it more bitter than they might have wished. Among those who protested was Nora Eddington Black, Flynn's second wife. She had divorced Flynn to marry Dick Haymes, and after that marriage failed, she wed Beverly Hills businessman Richard Black. She wrote to the *Los Angeles Times*:

> I was married to Errol Flynn for seven years, the first three of which were the last years of the Second World War. I make this point because of the allegations made by Charles Higham in his book *Errol Flynn: The Untold Story*. Errol was a wild spirit and about as unconventional as any man ever born. He hated authority, particularly policemen, and so the idea of him being attracted to the Nazis is absurd. One of the good things about Errol was that he was very communicative, he loved to talk and in our time together I heard about every detail of his life and all that he loved and hated. There was never the slightest hint of him being a supporter of the Nazis, in fact if he hated anyone, he would refer to him as a blankety-blank Nazi. Errol even resented being told what to do by Warner Bros. Can

anyone seriously imagine him wanting to live under a dictatorship?

I resent Higham's book because it is a fraud. He hasn't come up with a single document about Errol's supposed tie-in with the Gestapo, but he continues to go around the country saying he has. When he was working on his book, he came to me for information, which I gave him. Now I wish I hadn't, because he never revealed to me that he was taking this approach. I speak for Errol's other friends who are also quoted in the book. None of us realized that what we said would be used in a book of this kind.

If all the Nazi secret service files were captured, I would think that any prominent person who worked for them would be revealed. Dr. Hermann Erben, who was an old friend of Errol and the man around whom this whole Nazi connection seems to be based, has said over and over that Errol was not engaged in espionage. Higham just dismisses that.

Higham never even met Errol. In his book he says that Errol was never on any USO tours. In 1944 I saw Errol off when he went to Alaska (with Bob Hope) for six weeks to entertain the troops. He was also on a bond tour that year. If the rest of the facts in Higham's book are as solid as these, he should get some kind of prize.

I would also like people to know that Sir William Stephenson, who was the chief of British Intelligence, has said that Errol was not a German spy. Maybe Higham thinks Sir William doesn't know anything either.

NORA EDDINGTON BLACK

No matter how impassioned the protests of ex-wives and friends, they have no legal bearing. If the Flynn matter was to be cleared then much more weighty evidence needed to be marshalled. After the Higham-Flynn book emerged, I was curious to find out if these charges of espionage and treason had any credence. Knowing as much as I had learned about this complicated man, I would not have been greatly surprised at anything he might have done, although treason seemed a bit excessive. The obvious first place to seek clarification on this matter would be the FBI. They replied:

UNITED STATES DEPARTMENT OF JUSTICE
FEDERAL BUREAU OF INVESTIGATION
Washington, D.C. 20535
June 5, 1980.

For your information, the files of the FBI do contain information on Mr. Flynn which was released to Mr. Higham and others under the provisions of the Freedom of Information Act. Any conclusions reached by Mr. Higham were no doubt based on his review of these records, as well as documents obtained from other Federal Government agencies. While Errol Flynn was either the victim or the subject of several investigations conducted by the FBI, none were based on alleged espionage activities and no information was developed during these inquiries to indicate that he had been a Nazi agent. There are, however, numerous references to his name in the files of other individuals with whom he was associated and who were investigated by the FBI for alleged espionage activities.

DAVID G. FLANDERS,
Chief,
Freedom of Information—Privacy Acts Branch,
Records Management Division.

It seemed to me that this FBI report puts its finger on the Flynn problem—guilt by association. Flynn was a capricious man by nature and none too careful about his associations; he was drawn like a moth to flame to anything bizarre or dangerous. Still, I needed to know more. In regard to wartime espionage, the place to go was United States Army Intelligence.

The files of the SS and the Gestapo were captured shortly before the end of the war, and in addition to those files the Army also had access to the files of the OSS, the State Department and the Navy. In a letter dated May 6, 1980, and signed by Thomas P. Conley, Chief, Freedom of Information/Privacy Office, Department of the Army, U.S. Army Intelligence and Security Command, Fort George G. Meade, Maryland 20755, the information conveyed that there was no reference to Errol Flynn in any of their files. A year later, Mr. Conley amended that letter with another to the effect that they had discovered a reference to Flynn. It pertained to an inquiry from FBI Chief J. Edgar Hoover, addressed to the head of his Los Angeles Bureau—and it is a letter that is vital in unraveling the Flynn mystery:

June 22, 1942

Special Agent in Charge,
Los Angeles, California.

Re: ERROL FLYNN
SELECTIVE SERVICE

Dear Sir:

The following excerpt appeared in the column, "THESE CHARMING PEOPLE," by Igor Cassini, and was published in the *Washington Times Herald* on June 19, 1942.

"Errol Flynn, who was deferred by his Hollywood draft board because of a heart condition (sic). Funny that this should happen to the hero of the greatest screen battles, to the tennis champion of the movie colony, to the ex-boxer and to the greatest athlete of all Hollywood. Flynn's friends, however, say that he's burned up about criticism and that he wants to get into the Army at all costs. We'll see. Errol looks healthier to us than many men they take every day. If it's his heart that is weak, Flynn should have been buried long ago."

It is desired that you immediately check the records of the Local Selective Service Board covering the residence of Errol Flynn and review Flynn's Selective Service file. You should furnish the Bureau with the complete facts concerning Flynn's deferment within seven days.

This inquiry should be conducted in a very discreet manner, so that the fact it is being made will not be publicized.

Very truly yours,

JOHN EDGAR HOOVER
Director.

The Los Angeles office of the FBI replied to Hoover on July 3, 1942. The copy of the letter sent by U.S. Army Intelligence is censored in regard to names:

(BLANK), clerk of Local Draft Board No. 246, Beverly Hills, California, advised that the subject had been disqualified for military service by the United States Army Examining Board because of tuberculosis, and therefore had been placed in a IV-4 classification by the local board. (BLANK) advised that (BLANK) was chairman of the local board, and that (BLANK) and (BLANK) were the members of Local Board No. 246 and had been the members in their respective positions since the inception of the board.

The subject's Selective Service file was obtained from (BLANK) and it reflected on February 2, 1942, the subject was disqualified for military service by reason of "tuberculosis (sic), pulmonary, chronic reinfection (adult), type in the right apex." His physical examination was signed by (BLANK), examining physician.

Photographic copies were made of the subject's Selective Service file, and two copies are being forwarded to the Bureau. One photographic copy of this file and the negatives are being retained in the instant file in the Los Angeles Field Office. Subject's file was returned to Local Board No. 246 on July 1, 1942.

In view of the fact that there appears to be no violation of the Selective Training and Service Act in the subject's deferment, no further investigation will be conducted unless requested by the Bureau.

Apparently no further action was taken by Hoover upon receipt of that report. What makes Hoover's letter of vital interest in studying any possible involvement by Flynn in espionage is that Flynn had been tracked by the FBI, on Hoover's orders, for years because of concern about his sex life. The powerful but very puritanical head of the FBI regarded Flynn as a playboy degenerate and had him trailed whenever he left California, especially on trips to Mexico. Hoover suspected him of being involved in white slave trafficking and he was forever trying to nab Flynn on the Mann Act, the taking of girls across state lines for immoral purposes.

Early in 1940, Hoover instructed Special Agent Richard B. Hood to bear down on his Hollywood contacts for the purpose of reporting on anything that might be unflattering to the national image. Wars always produce heightened senses of patriotism and free-floating anxiety about morality on the visible and inspirational level. Hoover in the war years was an embodiment of these values, with a proclivity for celebrity indiscretions. Many years later that tendency would again become apparent in his attempts to smear Martin Luther King, Jr. During the Second World War, Hoover was in his element in this regard and the eventual torpedoing of Flynn on the rape charges probably grew from Hoover's disgust with the actor, and perhaps the frustration of not being able to nail him with the Mann Act. Flynn was reported to be a frequenter of one of the Los Angeles salons in which girls suspected of being recruited on that act were employed. When Flynn took Nora Eddington to Mexico in August of 1943, he was tracked by the FBI. Many reports were filed before the incident was cut short by the couple's marriage.

It is quite possible that no Hollywood actor during those years was more closely watched by the FBI than Errol Flynn. For that reason, it is reasonable to assume that no Hollywood actor was less likely than he to be involved in espionage and go unreported. Flynn did, in fact, have some contact with Germans during 1940, none of which went undetected.

One of the sticks with which Charles Higham beats Flynn in *The Untold Story* is the actor's socializing with Fritz Wiedermann, the German Consul General in San Francisco. As a British subject,

Flynn should not have contacted a German official after September 1939, but since he did it in a neutral country, it was not an overtly treasonable act unless later proven to be. What Higham does not allude to in *The Untold Story* is that Fritz Wiedermann was not a fervent Nazi. He had supported Hitler during Hitler's rise to power, but after the outbreak of war, he was among the many German diplomats and officials who had grave doubts about Germany's embarking on what seemed like another world war. Wiedermann was an Anglophile and he was soon consorting with his British counterparts in America to bring about a cessation of the conflict between Germany and Britain. It was Wiedermann who warned the British of Hitler's plans to attack Russia, a warning which they ignored. Later, when he advised them that Hitler planned to seal up both ends of the Mediterranean, they paid attention, and the British aid to the Yugoslavians came as a result, a campaign which proved to be a crippling irritation to the Germans. As a reward, the British shunted Wiedermann off to China, where he sat out the war.

Fritz Wiedermann, who claimed to be a German monarchist, also told the British of the underground resistance to Hitler in Germany and of proposed plots to kill him. If Wiedermann discussed any of this with Flynn, and there is no evidence one way or the other, I can imagine Flynn being highly excited with the prospect of involvement. It was before his trip to South America, presumably on behalf of the British Ministry of Propaganda, and the prospect of serving the cause probably pleased Flynn more than anything else he could have imagined. However, I am here allowing my research to fit my thesis—an ever present danger in speculating on the possible motives of the deceased, especially one as perplexing as Errol Flynn.

Charles Higham donated his Flynn research and documentation to the Doheny Library of the University of Southern California, Los Angeles, with the understanding it could be reviewed by any qualified journalist or film student. He asked that he be advised of whoever wished to see the material, but that restriction was eventually lifted since it did not comply with university standards and practices. In April of 1989, I spent four days examining the collection.

In *Cary Grant: The Lonely Heart*, Flynn figures so prominently because of espionage and treason charges that the authors list him in the index as a Nazi agent, and in apparent support of all these allegations, it is stated in the reference section of the book that "the massive Errol Flynn files at USC, drawn from every branch of the government, supply the full record of Flynn's and Erben's treason to the United States."

If the USC collection constitutes Higham's complete research papers on Flynn, then his claim that they supply a full record of treason is specious. I am willing to stand corrected if wrong, but from my own review of these papers, I cannot share Higham's conclusions. The use of the word *massive* is subjective. It is not one I would use in this regard. The material is contained in seven cardboard boxes, each about one foot by a foot and a half, and a foot deep. The material specifically about Flynn could fit into one box, the rest being about Erben and others. Large amounts of material are illegible due to being xerox copies of old, deteriorated photostats and many other documents are rendered useless by the censorial blacking out of names.

I could not find one document in this collection by which Errol Flynn could be specifically regarded as having been involved in treasonable acts against the United States. Aside from the one charge of aiding the Japanese during the making of *Dive Bomber*, based entirely on a quoted comment from a deceased producer, the remainder of the allegations revolved around Hermann Erben, with a few other documents alluding to Flynn's meetings with several Germans—with no confirmation of espionage acts.

In 1981, Dell Publishing brought out the paperback version of *Errol Flynn: The Untold Story*, having reportedly paid $400,000 for the rights. The cover, again superimposing a likeness of Flynn over a swastika, promised "shocking new documentary evidence never before published." Higham added an epilogue in which he discussed the reaction to the first edition and an appendix listing excerpts from thirty-nine further documents. Again most of them deal with Hermann Erben.

Among the points at which Higham advises those in search of documentation to find affirmation is "the National Archives, where room 6E has the Errol Flynn cards with 'PSA' (Probable Subversive Activities) stamped on them in red..." The card file actually reads "Flynn, April 2, 1943, 800. 20211/1072. Possible subversive activities" and is not written in red ink. The file contains a confidential monograph by J. Edgar Hoover, Director of the FBI, entitled "General Intelligence Survey in the United States" (March 1943). It is a study of possible subversive activities by German-Americans, Japanese, Latin Americans, Communists and other groups. The last name, "Flynn," appears on page 41 as a Communist Party leader. Obviously the wrong Flynn.

Item No. 23 in this new listing of evidence is marked "FBI Report, San Francisco, May 18, 1940." The evidence Higham here lists is actually taken from two reports made by Special Agent L.A. Langille, dated May 18 and May 20. These are located at the National Archives in File 800.20211, F/4, Jacket No. 1. A crucial portion of Higham's quotation reads that Erben "is becoming more and more anti-British and pro-German in his utterances and has repeatedly indicated his belief that the Nazi Armed Forces will prevail..."

The entire quotation from which the above is lifted reads: "Dr. Erben, it was observed, is becoming more and more anti-British and pro-German in his utterances and has repeatedly indicated his belief that the Nazi Armed Forces will prevail in the present European conflict, unless the United States becomes a party. Dr. Erben has repeatedly stated in recent interviews that if the United States enters the war, he will immediately endeavor to enlist in the United States Army, indicating that although he still feels that his German

9

blood is something of which he can be proud, he considers his first allegiance to the United States."

Although I am not about to be swayed by the sentiments expressed by Erben in the above, the full quotation does put him in a somewhat better light than the partial Higham quotation. The art of partial quotation is an insidious one and it can be used against anyone, even Charles Higham. For instance, in *Contemporary Authors*, Higham claims, "I have discovered, rather in middle life, a gift for fiction. This has been the greatest joy of my life." I shall, of course, resist all temptation to use that comment out of context.

In the appendix to the Dell edition of his Flynn book, Higham alludes to crucial OSS records on Flynn and claims, "The existence of the OSS records has been confirmed by British intelligence officers of the Ministry of Defense in London." In checking that claim in Washington, I received this reply:

National Archives,
Washington, DC 20408
July 14, 1989.

Dear Mr. Thomas:

The names of Hermann F. Erben and Errol Flynn do not appear in the name index to the Records of the Research and Analysis Branch of the Office of Strategic Services (OSS).

Sincerely,
JOHN E. TAYLOR
Military Reference Branch
Textual Reference Division.

Charles Higham also claims, "The Abwehr files on Flynn, captured by a double agent from Hamburg in 1943, are retained by the Ministry of Defense in London." The Ministry refuses to make any comment on that charge. And since Higham has never presented any documentation on Flynn's involvement with German military intelligence, how and why would Flynn have appeared in Abwehr records? If the British government have evidence of treasonable activity, why was no action ever taken against the actor?

My research associate in Washington, Lee A. Gladwin, spent several days at the National Archives examining German wartime documents. "Robert Wolfe was most helpful in guiding me through the inventories of German Captured Documents, and I looked through several of the cross-referenced Abwehr agent card files prepared by our Naval Intelligence at the end of the war. Specifically, the records belong to the OKW (Oberkommando Der Wehrmacht—German Armed Forces High Command), Amt Ausland/Abwehr—Abwehrnebenstelle Bremen, or Office of Foreign and Counter Intelligence, headquartered in Bremen. The original records were returned to West Germany. Naval Intelligence went through all of these documents and attempted to identify agents by code name, actual name and country of origin.

"Despite the extensiveness of these files, there is no mention of Flynn or Erben. The files themselves are on microfilm and available in the reading room on the fourth floor. From my studies of these files, I would have to conclude that there is no supportive evidence from the best sources available to prove Erben was an agent prior to the time he testified that he became one in 1941. As for Flynn's involvement with German government agencies of that period, there appears to be no evidence of any kind."

Of the thirty-nine pieces of additional evidence in the Dell version of *The Untold Story*, the most damaging toward Flynn would appear to be item No. 27, in which it appears the actor met with female German agents in Mexico. This is the version as printed in *The Untold Story*:

Department of State. Foreign Activity Correlation. January 18, 1943.

. . . VD (Visa Division)—Mr. Alexander.

Your particular attention is invited to attached telephone inter-

cept SATP 9891 from Errol Flynn to (BLANK). F.C. understands
that Flynn was recently in Mexico at which time he associated with
(BLANK), German national and suspected enemy agent. Visa Division may desire to consider most carefully the visa application of
(BLANK).

(Signed) W.H.A. COLEMAN

To the above, Charles Higham has added a footnote: "The 'German national and suspected enemy agent' is a woman, still living,
whose name cannot be revealed because of the Privacy Act." As used
by Higham, this is one of the most serious of his charges against
Flynn. It is also one of the most meretricious. The actual FBI
document uses names and not blanks:

Jan. 18, 1943
VD—Mr. Alexander:

Your particular attention is invited to attached intercept SATP
9891 from Errol Flynn to Linda P. Welter. FC understands that Flynn
was recently in Mexico at which time he associated with Hilda
Kruger (alias Miliza Korjus?) German national and suspected enemy
agent.

VD may desire to consider most carefully the visa application of
Linda P. Welter.

W. H.W. COLEMAN

With the use of names and not blanks the document is not
difficult to understand. The actual intercept, SATP, is one of three
documents in the Records of the Office of Censorship, RG 216,
Judicial and Fiscal Branch of the National Archives. It would appear that Flynn was simply arranging a film contract for another of
his conquests and trying to expedite a visa. Linda P. Welter became
known as film actress Linda Christian and it was Flynn who got her
to Hollywood. In her own book, *Linda, My Story* (Crown, 1962), she

relates how Flynn called her in Mexico City nearly every evening. Since she was of German parentage and since the FBI were very concerned about German activity in Mexico, she came under surveillance.

The document's confusion regarding the names of Hilda Kruger and Miliza Korjus is typical of wartime espionage surveillance in that it errs on the side of the government. Such documentation is full of errors and assumptions, not unnaturally in view of wartime tensions and desperation. Polish-born Miliza Korjus was a noted soprano with the Berlin Opera during the 1920s and 1930s and was brought to Hollywood by MGM in 1937 to star in *The Great Waltz.* She never appeared in another Hollywood film but afterwards concertized and accepted offers to make films in Mexico, which is what she was doing in 1943. There was never any question of Korjus being a Nazi sympathizer.

Hilda Kruger was a German actress who came to Hollywood in 1939 to break into the movies but met with no success. Flynn met her in San Francisco at the time he also met Fritz Wiedermann. The German Consul General and Kruger were close friends, if not lovers, and their association brought Kruger under FBI surveillance, and by periphery Flynn as well. In 1941, Kruger went to Mexico City to make films and Flynn doubtlessly visited her. Kruger was a woman who enjoyed moving in the society of the rich and the famous, diplomats included—she even claimed Anthony Eden as a friend— but she denied ever having been involved in espionage and she was never charged. She and Korjus were confused in several FBI and State Department documents, making it difficult to know just which one Flynn was supposed to have met as noted in the January 18, 1943, letter. But there is no question that the letter mainly deals with Flynn and his plans to get Linda P. Welter into the movies— and he claimed that calling her Linda Christian was his invention.

All the palaver about Errol Flynn being or not being a Nazi sympathizer and agent would probably have died down once the Higham book had run its course. But it is Higham himself who has kept the matter alive. Flynn has been a figure in most of the books Higham has written since 1980.

In *Princess Merle: The Romantic Life of Merle Oberon* (Coward-Mc-Cann, 1983), written with Roy Mosely, Higham claims that Flynn expressed such great and vocal admiration for Hitler and the Nazis at a party in Mayfair, London, in 1933 that the British government began a file on him. A prominent British actress was then asked by that government to keep an eye on Flynn. The authors ask, "Could it have been Merle?" My reaction is to ask why. How could the opinions of an unknown, recently arrived young Aussie have merited such attention? And would that young man, then trying so hard to break into the London theatre and the film business, have made such noise about the German Chancellor? The so-called Mayfair Fascism of the pre-war years has been well covered in a number of books, in none of which does Flynn rate a mention. Merle Oberon claimed that she met Flynn only once, in Mexico City, but Higham and Mosely aver that the subject of their book was mistaken. Since Oberon had been dead for four years by the time they wrote their book, it is difficult to understand how the authors can be so sure about her forgetfulness.

In *Sisters: The Story of Olivia de Havilland and Joan Fontaine* (Coward-McCann, 1984), Charles Higham alludes to Olivia not understanding why her co-star in *Santa Fe Trail* (1940) was extremely tense and nervous, "She couldn't understand it, but the reason was that the FBI was constantly following him, checking up on his secretly known Nazi connections..." If this is true, and Flynn knew he was being tailed, then the FBI agents were doing a poor job of what should have been a furtive operation. Says Olivia de Havilland, in response to my questioning her about this: "The reactions attributed to me by Charles Higham are as absurd as they are false. I have no recollection of Errol being tense or nervous on that film. My problems with him at that time were purely personal. He deliberately and provocatively upstaged me in two scenes, something he had never done before... and since then I have wondered if his behavior might have had something to do with the fact that I was at the time seeing a lot of Jimmy Stewart and that our affable co-star Ronald Reagan spent a lot of time talking with me on the set. Since Errol was still married to Lili Damita, albeit unhappily, he was hardly in a position to court me but I knew he was fond of me, as I was of him. Someone else paying attention to me seemed to bother him a bit."

After Flynn died, Olivia de Havilland was asked by the press for comment. One of her stories received wide attention:

> A couple of years before he died, I had an unhappy experience in Hollywood. A tall man kissed me on the back of the neck at a party and I whirled around in anger and said, "Do I know you?" Then I realized it was Errol. He had changed so. His eyes were so sad. I had stared into them in enough movies to know his spirit was gone.

This is how that encounter appears in the pages of *Sisters: The Story of Olivia de Havilland and Joan Fontaine*:

> She also had a ghastly experience at a party. Someone touched her on the shoulder, saying her name, and she spun around, expecting to see an old friend, and saw instead a fat, bloated, horribly depraved-looking man with liquor on his breath, bloodshot eyes and a double chin. She froze, and the man walked off, looking dejected. Only later did Olivia discover that the man was Errol Flynn. She started to cry when she was told.

Olivia de Havilland's comment on the above: "I am really shocked at Higham's account of my impressions of Errol during our last meeting, which was at the Costumer's Ball in 1957. Errol was still a handsome man and rather lean. His eyes were certainly not bloodshot, he did not have a double chin and he was not depraved looking. Instead, he seemed, though as tall as ever, somehow sad and diminished within himself, and it was this self, looking out at me through those once merry eyes of his, that I did not recognize. The mischief was gone."

Like David Niven, Olivia de Havilland believes that Flynn's lack of success in getting into the services in wartime, or to be able to serve in any direct way while at the same time playing pre-posterously heroic roles in films, embarrassed him. "It was obvious to all of us who knew him that he was frustrated," she told us. "I saw Errol in either May or June of 1942 in Washington, D.C., where he had gone to discuss what he thought would be his usefulness. He was dining alone at Harvey's restaurant, and when he had finished his meal, he came over to the table where I was having supper with John Huston. Errol seemed in an intense, serious mood and smoked a lot. He didn't talk about why he was in the capital but it all came out in the papers afterwards, together with the news that he had been turned down on physical grounds by the armed services. I think this was a great blow to him and that later he felt deeply frustrated at not being able to serve in the war in some other significant way.

"Errol was a proud, sensitive man, and though every bit as adventurous as his screen roles, I think he was rather more complex than these. His own view of himself suffered several shocks within a short space of time in 1942 and 1943, and I think he never recovered from them. The rejection of the U.S. Government was one, and the other was the tawdry lawsuits by the young women who brought against him claims of statutory rape. His self-esteem was damaged permanently by these events, I do believe, and as the years rolled on his subsequent behavior became almost self punishing."

Flynn also turns up in Higham's *Orson Welles: The Rise and Fall of an American Genius* (St. Martin's Press, 1985). There is a passing reference to Flynn's "crucial role in fascist activities in Europe and the Americas," and a longer one due to Flynn having rented his yacht *Zaca* to Welles for filming *The Lady From Shanghai* (1948). Muses Higham, "How ironical that Welles, a liberal, would want to do business with Flynn, whose role in the Spanish Civil War, unbeknownst to Welles, was just the opposite of that taken by the Irish loyalist sailor whom Welles would portray in the film."

In *Trading With the Enemy* (Delacorte Press, 1983), Higham spots Flynn as a friend of the American industrialist-millionaire Charles Bedaux, a Nazi collaborator. "In the summer of 1937, according to MI-6 files in the Ministry of Defence, London, Bedaux met with the Duke of Windsor, Bedaux's close friend, Errol Flynn, Rudolf Hess and Martin Bormann in a secret encounter in the Hotel Meurice in Paris." How any movie star as visible as Flynn, to say nothing of the Duke, Hess and Bormann, could keep a secret encounter in a hotel as conspicuous as the Meurice and not be spotted by the press is a mystery—except that it is a mystery that can be explained.

Flynn arrived back in New York from his 1937 trip to Europe on April 19. He proceeded by train to Los Angeles, where he was already overdue on his next film, *The Perfect Specimen*. Shooting began on May 14 and lasted until July 14. Flynn was kept on hand for pick-up shots, the last one of which was done on August 19. He then went into pre-production for *The Adventures of Robin Hood*, spending the first few weeks studying archery with champion Howard Hill. Filming began in the middle of September and involved Flynn for more than two months.

It was not only Flynn who was not in Paris in the summer of 1937. Neither was the Duke of Windsor. After their marriage on June 3, 1937, the Windsors honeymooned for three months in Austria. On September 9, they visited Charles Bedaux, who was then living in Hungary. Bedaux persuaded the Windsors to make a tour of Germany to observe labor and housing conditions, which they did in October, and during the course of which they met the likes of Hess and Bormann. The Windsors made an appearance in Paris before the German tour, on September 27. It would appear that the files of MI-6 are as questionable as those of the secret services of any other country.

Another 1937 mystery: In *The Untold Story* Higham writes, "The Ministry of Defence made a startling revelation about Flynn's connection with Sean Russell, head of the Irish Republican Army, for whom Flynn named his son. Russell was tracked to a secret meeting with Flynn in a hotel in Lisbon in August, 1937." In his book *American Swastika* (Doubleday, 1985), Higham writes, "Flynn was traced, by agents of MI-6, to a meeting with Russell at a hotel in Lisbon in May, 1938." I cannot account for Flynn's activities in May of 1938—he was on leave between making the films *Four's a Crowd* and *The Sisters*—but it is my guess that he was cruising his ketch *Sirocco* in the waters off Catalina Island, and not hauling himself by 1938 transportation to Portugal. And one wonders if perhaps there were not other IRA supporters by the name of Flynn.

The idea of Flynn going to bat for the Irish Republican Army strikes me as far from credible. The one true allegiance of Flynn's life was his father, who spent the last twenty years of his academic life in Belfast. Professor Theodore Thomson Flynn was a true-blue Aussie Britisher, whose greatest pride came from being awarded the Order of the British Empire for his wartime services in civil defence in Northern Ireland. He went to Buckingham Palace to accept the OBE from King George VI. His Hollywood son would have to wait until 1949 before being presented to the Monarch.

In 1967, while researching *The Films of Errol Flynn*, I accepted an invitation to visit his sister Rosemary in Washington, D.C., where she lived with her husband Charles Warner. Theodore Thomson Flynn was staying with her at that time; he had recently lost is wife, Marelle, in a car accident in Brighton, England, and he was now in the last year of his own life. I was charmed by the old gentleman. He was a little doddery and his attention drifted as we talked about his son. He wanted to talk about himself and every now and again he would leave the room and return with another of his citations and honors, including the OBE. When I told him I was writing a book about his son, he smiled and wished me luck, adding that perhaps he should write one himself, once he figured out his "enigmatic Errol." Later in a letter to me, he wrote, "Errol and I were very close. I loved him greatly and any differences we had were due to the fact that to my mind he did not take sufficient care in the selection of some of the people he knew. He was very unjust to himself."

In Charles Higham's best-selling book *The Duchess of Windsor: The Secret Life* (McGraw Hill, 1988) Flynn is fleetingly referred to twice. First as being one of Adolf Hitler's idols, which, if true, is in odd counterpoint to Flynn's 1937 book *Beam Ends* being banned in Germany as unfit for the minds of German youth. In the second reference he is an "egregious movie star with extensive Nazi connections," keeping a politically nefarious rendezvous in the Bahamas in 1941. However, in *Cary Grant: The Lonely Heart*, a 1989 best-seller, Flynn, the Nazi, looms large.

Authors Higham and Mosely once again take us back to Spain in 1937, but this time Hermann Erben ceases to be an Austrian and becomes a German, with much reference to his passionate dedication to Nazism. The book reveals that Cary Grant performed wartime services for British Intelligence and because of it he knew about Flynn's purported treason. They quote a gentleman named Joseph Longstreth as having been told by Grant that Grant exposed Flynn to the authorities as a Nazi agent and collaborator but that it was decided to do nothing about it. Higham and Mosely suggest that Grant probably learned about Flynn from Noel Coward, the British entertainer who was most deeply involved with undercover work for the British government during the Second World War. Certainly Coward knew a great deal, but if he knew Flynn to be a traitor, would he have socialized with him later? Would not Flynn have been held in contempt by such a man as Coward?

In *The Noel Coward Diaries* (Little Brown, 1982), the entry for March 27, 1951, written in Jamaica, reads: "In the evening dined with Errol Flynn and his wife Pat. Drinks on his yacht which is beautiful, then barbecue dinner on his island—palm trees—lit by torches. Both of them extremely nice; a really lovely evening." Coward and Flynn were neighbors for some years in Jamaica, and I can speak from personal experience having visited both their homes, in Port Antonio and Port Maria, respectively.

Higham and Mosely believe the reason Grant never spoke out against Flynn was that Flynn was possibly of more value to the war effort as a movie hero than as a defendant in an espionage trial, which, if true, would make Flynn the only known traitor of prominence never brought to justice. Higham's former claim that Flynn drove Erben across the Mexican border on November 15, 1940, is here reduced to having provided him with a rental car. However, the authors of the Grant book further indict Flynn as being involved with his fellow Aussie, playboy friend Freddie McEvoy, in smuggling guns, drugs and tungsten. On the subject of Flynn's treason, they conclude, "So complete was Flynn's power as a film star that nothing seemed to affect his popularity, even in a movie colony dominated by Jews."

If Cary Grant knew about Flynn as a Nazi agent, why did he never allude to it publicly after Flynn's death? Grant and Flynn were never friends but they met at Hollywood social and industry functions, and Grant was never seen to shun Flynn—as a man probably would if he knew the other was a traitor to a cause he himself had defended. Grant might have touched upon the matter, even accidentally, when he was interviewed by Sheridan Morley for the book Morley wrote about David Niven, *The Other Side of the Moon* (Harper and Row, 1985). In talking about the differences in style between himself and Niven, Grant said his own was derived from the British comedians of the 1920s London stage, "whereas I think David was far more impressed with the movie people like Flynn." Morley is also the author of *Tales from the British Raj*, in which he explores the days of the extensive British colony in Hollywood, with emphasis on the war years in which the California Brits rallied around the Union Jack. Morley points out that Flynn was never a part of that mostly English group, but in talking to the survivors, Morley picked up nothing on Flynn other than that the playboy Errol was considered too frivolous in his lifestyle to be taken seriously by the Hollywood Cricket Club.

The Flynn-Higham brushfire flared up again in Los Angeles in February of 1989 with a story in the *Times* that Flynn's friend, Buster Wiles, had written a recollection, *My Days With Errol Flynn*

(Roundtable, 1989), in collaboration with William Donati, who added an appendix of his own to the book, giving a lengthy rebuttal to the Higham charges. Donati claimed that Higham had not only altered government documents but that he had illegally rewritten several Warner Brothers memos. *Los Angeles Times* reporter Pat Broeske asked Higham for a comment and got it. "I wonder why we are talking about this at all. The Flynn case is closed. My book was exhaustively documented. I would stress to you that I am a serious person and a serious scholar."

Higham's claim that "the case on Errol Flynn is closed" struck me as sheer arrogance, since the only case is the one he had created. I wrote a letter to the *Los Angeles Times* making that point, and in the same issue of the paper, there appeared a letter from a gentleman in New York:

I note Higham states his book was "exhaustively documented." Having known Flynn and carefully read Higham's book, I recall Higham's many talk show appearances, wherein he stated that documentation of his assertions and charges in his book were en route from England and elsewhere. These statements were repeated on several talk shows. I would like to know if the so-called documentation has arrived. If so, where is it?

JOHNATHEN CAVENDISH

The letters brought an angry response from Higham:

After my book on Errol Flynn appeared in 1979, numerous eye witnesses came forward, including a now prominent film preservationist, a former Flynn secretary, a distinguished San Francisco lawyer, an MI5 official and a leading MGM producer to confirm my findings that Flynn was a collaborator with the Germans. Yet there are still those die-hards who insist upon Flynn's innocence in the face of all the available evidence.

Evidence . . . and the Lack Thereof

Tony Thomas and William Donati have been among the more vocal skeptics. They have based their conclusions largely upon statements made to them by Flynn's intimate friend and fellow Nazi, the late Dr. Hermann Erben. This former SA and SD member is the preferred source of these journalists.

I have better sources. Letter writer Johnathen Cavendish seems to question the existence of these. They are to be found not in the FBI files but in the State Department Foreign Activities Correlation (Intelligence Branch), Naval Intelligence, Military Intelligence, Censorship Office and Flynn-Erben correspondence files presently housed at the USC Doheny Library. They may be examined by qualified scholars.

The core documents in the safe include Flynn's letter of Sept. 22, 1933, addressed to Erben, who had, by his own admission to me, inculcated Flynn into the Nazi philosophy. The letter includes the words: "I do wish we could bring Hitler over here (England) to teach these Isaacs a thing or two."

CHARLES HIGHAM

If, as Higham claims, Erben admitted to him that he inculcated Flynn into Nazism, the admission would have had to have been made by telephone since Higham and Erben never met, and the admission is at variance with Erben's comments on the subject with other interviewers.

The excerpt from the Flynn letter to Erben is correct but it needs to be considered in the context of the whole. Most of the letter is personal, dealing with the pursuit of work or women. But in one section he tells Erben about hiring a Jewish firm to help him retrieve some lost property and that he felt they were cheating him out of half the proceeds. "The bastards have absolutely no business probity or honor whatsoever." It is a tasteless comment by a rash young man but hardly one to brand him as a rabid anti-Semite or someone believing that Nazism was the answer to the ills of the world. And since this is the only letter from Flynn in the USC

165

collection pertaining to that period—to Erben or anybody else—it is barely reason enough for Higham to claim, "In England, Flynn had written passionately pro-Hitler letters, including one in which he stated he would like to see the Führer in Britain to take care of the Jews."

My own book *From a Life of Adventure: The Writings of Errol Flynn* came out at the same time as Higham's Flynn book. I sent a copy of mine to Hermann Erben as a means of winning his interest and attention. I had an ulterior motive. I had received permission from the Canadian Broadcasting Corporation, for whom I was at that time acting as a Hollywood correspondent, to fly to Vienna to film Erben for a television interview. I explained to Erben that it was not my purpose to defend Flynn—the movie idol had long been gone—I wanted the truth and that if the actor had really been engaged in supporting the Nazis it would make for a riveting story. However, my plans were short-lived because a few days later, ABC announced that they were sending a team to Vienna to interview Erben for "20/20." The story was hardly worth coverage by two networks.

Despite all that I had learned about Erben, about his obvious zeal for Hitler and the Nazi cause, and about his contemptuous regard for American governmental procedures, causing him to lose his citizenship, to say nothing of his duplicity in wartime, I was touched by the tone of his letter to me:

Dannebergplatz 19/17,
A-1030 Vienna, Austria.
June 29, 1980.

Dear Mr. Thomas:

With your book on Errol you certainly have made me very happy, many thanks for sending it. It brings vividly back to me the boy I met in Rabaul in New Guinea in 1933, whom I was able to assist to get out of New Guinea and with whom I returned to Marseilles in a prolonged, leisurely trip, calling at all the ports that interested us. Hong Kong, Saigon and Colombo, a side trip to India and Madura, another break in at that time French Somali-Land Djibuti and finally via Italy to Marseilles.

Thus I met the young Flynn, a boy just on the brink of developing into a man. Despite of the hardships and disappointments New Guinea had been for him he wasn't bitter, had made the best of his bad luck and by the end of this very long and interesting voyage I learned to respect and admire this young British boy and a real friendship developed between us.

When I next met Flynn he had "made it," not only had he been in London at the Old Vic and tried his hand at the legitimate stage, a wish he had been toying with throughout the trip, but far more than that, he had skyrocketed and become a recognized star at Warner Brothers. What I found however was the same easy-going, life loving and enjoying Errol, who however remembered somewhat nostalgically our days in New Guinea, when he called me the old bush slang title "My good old Nurmunger," amongst his sophisticated new surroundings.

As if we sensed that our friendship would be terminated by political upheavals I spent as much time as possible with Errol when my ship would touch in at San Pedro. I stayed until my ship had to fly the "blue Peter (the flag of departure)," always with Errol and Lili and at the studios in Burbank. His and my longing to never miss any excitement in the world paid off. When I tried to persuade him to come with me to the civil war in Spain he enthusiastically agreed, much to the displeasure of Lili. But we went. On our way via London and Paris I discovered a new side in Errol's character. Typical of the Australian-born Britisher, he just loved the "Old Country" and in London he never stopped to remark on the old "Pommy" cars and how he loved dear old London. We went to Spain together and here again I noticed the compassion he was capable of. Throughout the times we were confronted with the tragedies of war and how men died for love of their own country, torn apart by political ideologies, still men of the same blood.

Many hours we talked together in the trenches. Flynn was a man with the keenest sense of observation and considered the civil war in Spain a great tragedy. Our talks convinced me all over again that Flynn was a man of sterling character. He had remained unspoiled by the colossal success he had made in Hollywood. He had remained fully himself, as I had known him from New Guinea on.

War had suddenly broken up our happy days together in Burbank. It was Wednesday, November 13th, 1940, the last day I was ever to see Errol, by that time the best friend I had ever had in my life. You can imagine how I felt when I was confronted in two Vienna newspapers on January 6th, 1980, that someone had taken it upon himself to smear viciously and cunningly the memory of a man.

Errol Flynn was my friend, no more and no less. To this I wish to add that despite of the rather short time counted in years that our friendship lasted I consider him unreservedly as one of my dearest and most understanding friends.

Looking forward to meeting you I once more wish to thank you for your kindness of sending me your book about Errol.

Sincerely yours,
HERMANN F. ERBEN, M.D

I never met Erben and after another letter or two there was no further contact. He lived for another five years and anyone else who visited him or wrote to him received the same response to the Higham-Flynn charges that I had received. There is much to question about Hermann Erben but his loyalty to Flynn was not in doubt. And by the same token, Charles Higham has never retreated from his belief that Errol Flynn was the Nazi agent and traitor he has steadfastly claimed him to be.

Flynn's daughters, Deirdre and Rory, attempted to sue Higham for what they felt he had done to their father's reputation. They hired a famed attorney with a grandstand style, Melvin Belli, who roared with righteous wrath that Flynn was as upstanding an American as Benjamin Franklin. Anyone standing in the vicinity of the Flynn grave at that moment might be forgiven for imagining they heard a guffaw from below. The case was quickly dismissed, with the California appeals court taking the stand that "defamation of a deceased person does not rise to a civil right of action at common law in favor of the surviving spouse, family or relatives who are not themselves defamed." In short, dead celebrities are fair game—as are authors who write books of sensational, controversial content.

In the collection Charles Higham donated to the Doheny Library of the University of Southern California, he included the manuscript of the additional material he wrote for the expanded paperback version of *The Untold Story*, including pages not used. A section he wisely decided not to use is this:

> Then Margo, Mrs. Eddie Albert, called up to say that during *The Roots of Heaven*, in Africa, Flynn had broken down and told Albert everything about his Nazi associations. She told several other friends about this and then panicked and withdrew.

I asked Eddie Albert for his response to this: "Nothing like that ever took place. I had a lot of fun with Errol doing *The Sun Also Rises* and *The Roots of Heaven*, but he never said anything about being involved with Nazis or anybody else. It was hard to get him to talk seriously about anything. And Margo certainly wouldn't have said anything bad about anyone's reputation. That was not her nature. Higham called me once a long time ago and I refused to speak to him. It's all a lot of horse shit."

Also in the USC collection is the manuscript page for the new ending Higham wrote for the paperback version of his book:

> The myth of Errol Flynn dies hard. For many people, no matter what the evidence, it will always be impossible to believe that the gallant, fun-loving Robin Hood could have been a traitor.

In the margin of his manuscript for the above there is a handwritten note to the editor: "Please don't alter last paragraph. I like it too well now!" It is not difficult to understand why the author should like that ending. It is skillfully phrased and seemingly provides a neat finish to a strange and bizarre story—except in the minds of those who believe that this strange and bizarre story of treason on the part of a legendary Hollywood star is itself a myth.

Epilogue

REBUTTAL FOR A FRIEND
by
PATRIC KNOWLES

Patric Knowles was twenty-five when he was brought from England by Warner Brothers to play Errol Flynn's younger brother in *The Charge of the Light Brigade* in 1936. A year or so later, Knowles played Will Scarlet in *The Adventures of Robin Hood*, followed by roles in two Flynn films of 1938, *Four's a Crowd* and *The Sisters*. He left Warners the next year to sign a long-term contract with Universal, a period broken by his wartime service with the Royal Canadian Air Force. Knowles later appeared in a wide range of films before opting for retirement by the end of the Sixties.

Errol Flynn was my friend. I liked him immensely; in fact you may substitute the word "loved" for liked. We have liked thousands of people during our lives. There was only one Errol—a man's man. I was his close companion for many years. He was my son's god-father. The christening mug he presented to my son bore the inscription, "What fortune were thine, Godson, had you but entered the world with a father like me." One day, at my house, I asked him what he had meant; he just looked over at my wife, Enid, and grinned his "Flynn grin"—that God awful, charming, secret grin that made the gals shiver. I thought *I* knew what he meant but I wondered if *he* knew what he meant.

I always felt so *alive* around Flynn. Every moment was used up in an exciting manner; never a dull moment.

I read his book *My Wicked, Wicked Ways*, and while I enjoyed it very much, there were many episodes he left untouched, enough, I should imagine, to fill another volume or two. Also, I had the feeling that he was giving his readers just what they wanted him to give them—sex, buckets and buckets full of sex. Knowing Flynn, I firmly believe he wrote every word of *My Wicked, Wicked Ways* with his tongue in a position other than dead center. I wish someone would discover the manuscript of the book he could and may have written. I wish it could be published so that his disclaimers might discover for themselves the other Flynn. The Flynn only a few close friends knew about. The "public Flynn," or perhaps I should say the Flynn in public, reminded me of a puppy—an overgrown, extremely healthy puppy, who, after being cooped up in a fenced-in kennel yard, happily discovers a hole in the fence and makes his escape. The world he discovered *outside* was so exciting he could hardly stand the ecstasy. The delights he found were so many and of such magnitude he barely had time to scrape the surface of each discovery. He hurriedly sniffed here—and then over there. Such a wide variety of things to do, wonderful and delightful things. He would run from pillar to post in a frenzy of eagerness, love and laughter. Sometimes he'd run full tilt into a post and hurt himself; he'd pause and wonder for a moment but he'd never blame the post for the hurt he had suffered.

He lived life as if it were a game—a game he enjoyed playing. But he was an impatient player—not to win, but to move along to the next bout.

Those, like myself, who came to know him well, fell quickly under the spell of his charm and good looks...the personality which, later on, prompted the saying, "In like Flynn."

He also had the luck of the Irish for sure...

We were on location at a place called Chico, in northern California. We were making *The Adventures of Robin Hood*. Flynn played the title role while I enacted the part of Will Scarlet, one of his merry men.

It was our custom, every morning, on returning to our hotel from filming, to stop by the small airfield outside Chico. The operator, Bill Miller, was a friend of ours and he was having a tough time (pardon the pun) getting his business off the ground. At that time (1937), I think he had a Piper Cub and an old Curtis Robin.

I had a total of fifty hours flying time and Flynn had none—solo time, I mean. Well, I talked him into learning how to fly the Cub and I'd like to mention at this point that it took twelve hours of dual instruction to solo yours truly—Flynn made it in four hours. Our studio (Warner Brothers) somehow found out about our flying every evening and we began to receive messages from various departments, warning us of the grave consequences should anything happen to us while flying. One note to me asked if I realized that I was endangering the life of the star of the picture and jeopardizing the investment of several millions of dollars. No one said anything about *my* life. We ignored all the notes and messages and continued to fly each evening until a telegram arrived. It was addressed to me and signed by the producer of the picture. It threatened me with some sort of legal action if I persisted in encouraging Flynn to fly.

I asked the "old boy" what we should do about the threat and he laughed loud and long, as they say. "Don't get yourself in an uproar, old son. Just tear up the telegram and forget about it."

I did, then we flipped a coin to see who would fly first. He won. "Why don't you have the driver put the car in the hangar, out of the way," he said. "Then the snoopers won't know whether we are here or not."

We hid the car in the back of the hangar while Flynn "flewed." I mean FLEWED. We phooled all over the sky, showing off. Nothing really dangerous—just hammer stalls, tight turns and wing overs. After only four hour dual, he was a veritable Rickenbacker.

He didn't say a word as he climbed out of the cockpit and I got in. He simply leered at me with a let's-see-what-you-can-do look. Well, I did everything but fly through the hangar doors. Then, to finish off, climbed up to a thousand feet and did two loops, landing at the end of the second one.

You can imagine the smug grin I was wearing as I got out of the plane. I didn't wear it for long. Two men were approaching. One man I knew; he was the production manager from the studio, the other was a stranger to me.

I'll wind it up fast for you. The stranger was a Civil Aeronautics Authority man. They had arrived on the field just as I took off and had witnessed my performance. The studio manager informed me that they were going to lodge a complaint with the Screen Actors Guild. The C.A.A. man took away my license pending the outcome of the hearing on my case at a later date. The charges? Flying in a manner to endanger the lives and property of the public. Stunting without a parachute.

Later, in the car, on the way to our hotel, I asked Flynn where he was during the excitement. "Why, in the car having forty winks, old son," he said. "I started to learn my lines for tomorrow and simply dozed off."

That's the sort of thing I mean when I say Flynn had the luck of the Irish. By the way, the Screen Actors Guild fined me one hundred dollars and my license was reinstated at the hearing by the C.A.A.

This story is titled "Rebuttal for a Friend," but if you think I'm going to say Flynn was a virgin, never used four-letter words, or drank intoxicating liquids—you're mistaken. (They don't hardly make any of them anymore.) What I am going to say is this ... Flynn never did anything vicious or hurtful to anyone in his entire life. There are some who will argue that point, of course, and so, to concede the fact that indirectly some people's lives were changed by Flynn's actions, I will add the word "knowingly."

Flynn was a motion picture star in the true sense. A fine physique, good looks and great charm. His studio spent millions of dollars publicizing his movies and, as a result, Flynn, too. The publicity department received instructions to "go all-out" on him after his first success. They did just that and they created a Flynn who simply didn't exist—until much later.

I was in Flynn's company on many occasions when a reporter or photographer encouraged him to enlarge on the truth in order to make the story or photograph conform to the "Flynn tradition." It didn't take Flynn long to fall into this pattern of *broadening* when interviewed by the press—they expected it of him. And I can say, from experience, that most of the stories written about people in the entertainment world are the results of press agents and publicity men eager to do a good job for their clients. Several times I have been the victim of an over-imaginative press agent. I remember a case in particular...

Flynn and I were under contract to Warners in England. Irving Asher, the head of the studio, was the one who sent Flynn to Hollywood and so, I would say, discovered Flynn. Anyway, when they were casting *The Charge of the Light Brigade* in Hollywood, they discovered they had no one to play the part of Flynn's brother. Irving Asher sent Jack Warner some film of mine and I was approved for the part.

Flynn and I renewed our acquaintance on location at Lone Pine, California, and became fast friends while making *The Charge*.

In those years, Flynn and I were supposed to look alike. Neither of us could see it though. Someone started the rumor that I had been brought to Hollywood strictly as a *threat* to Flynn. He had risen to the heights so quickly, they expected trouble from him and I was the studio's "pinch hitter."

I first heard of the rumor when a nationally syndicated columnist called me for an interview. I was quite inexperienced in the ways of answering questions in those days and the resulting statements I was supposed to have uttered were printed in all the newspapers in the country. I was embarrassed to say the least, but the "old boy" called me to say he liked the interview and I should always "keep it interesting" in future publicity.

Flynn knew he had no worries about my taking over from him. In the first place, in night clubs I'm a coward, but a live coward. I have enough trouble fighting the booze, never mind the customers. In the second place, "In like Knowles" doesn't rhyme.

I visited him on a film set a few months before he passed away. We talked of the old days, and when I left, he put his arm around my shoulder and said with a grin, "Let me know, old son, when you want to take over. I'm getting too old for this sort of thing." I knew him when he wasn't too old for anything. Like the time we were in Balboa, California...

Flynn, myself and three or four cronies were spending a weekend on his ketch *Sirocco*. We left the boat moored in the channel and went ashore to stretch our legs and visit one of the many pubs. All of us were fairly well known in the movies and word soon spread around that we were in Balboa at a certain tavern. Five or six teenage girls entered the place and demanded our autographs. We obliged them and invited them to join us in a soft drink.

Well, you know how things are. We sat around and had a good time talking to the girls for half an hour, then they left. Soon after, we departed. We intended to return to the boat and take a swim. But on the dock, waiting for us, were half a dozen of the biggest teenage football stars I ever want to see. As I mentioned before, I'm a live coward, and a couple of the other blokes weren't at all shy about retiring either. We ignored the small boat waiting to transport us back to the big boat and dove into the bay fully clothed. As we swam out, we could hear Flynn whooping away on the dock.

Epilogue

Looking back, Flynn was holding off the enemy and laughing while doing it. He was *enjoying* himself.

The kids finally drove him off the dock by sheer weight of numbers. He swam to the boat and as we dragged him aboard he gasped, ".Friends of the girls in the pub."

You know how that little episode appeared in the papers? "Flynn in Brawl Over Girls."

Many times, while in Flynn's company, I have seen some noble and brave types, full of "flit" usually, walk up to him and open with, "You're not so Goddam tough. I could take you with one arm tied behind my back." He'd say it in a loud voice, then turn around and shout to someone across the room. "See, honey. I did it." Then, encouraged by his success, he would press his luck further. Flynn would try to be patient. He'd "yes" the guy and sometimes buy him a drink. He often was forced to leave the premises.

We worked out a system to discourage the fight-pickers. It was this... if some showoff tried to start something, we'd separate a little and so arrange it that the bloke would be between us. Then, while the spook concentrated on Flynn, I filled his pocket full of ice cubes. Childish? It usually accomplished its purpose. Because, on signal, Flynn and I would retire a short way and observe the reaction when our friend became aware of the ice cubes in his pocket. Usually, his expression would change from that of a cocky showoff to one of a man who realizes he had made a damn fool of himself.

Flynn was generous to a fault and sometimes it annoyed me to see the way he was taken—even by close friends.

I almost took him for a hundred and sixty dollars once...

I was in Canada, with the RCAF, as a flying instructor. I had some leave coming so, like a flash, I headed for Hollywood. I caught up with Flynn at the Hotel del Coronado in San Diego, at the time he was making *Dive Bomber*. After hinting to him he invited me to visit him for a few days and, since he had a suite, said

I could stay with him. He worked all day and retired early to study his script for the next day's work. As a result, I didn't have much time with him. I was left to myself and, well, I spent all my money amusing myself. I was broke—not even enough to pay my fare back to the Canadian border. I mentioned the fact to Flynn.

I wrote to him later and thanked him for his generosity. He wrote in reply from San Diego:

My dear old bastard:

Thanks for your letter. I don't mind you going to my business manager. I don't mind you getting into him, or rather me, for one hundred and sixty clams—I don't mind a lot of other things about you, but I do wish when next you come to stay with me, you will not use all the towels in my bathroom, depriving me of any means of drying my glorious body, apart from the curtains. In short, you can go too far. This is particularly embarrassing when some little beauty with whom I am slightly acquainted and trying to impress, goes into the bathroom and has to wind up using the bath mat with which to dry her pretty, little face. What did you do with the towels? Are things that bad in Canada?

Old son, it was wonderful to see you, but particularly annoying not to have the least chance for one of those long gossips—philosophical, lewd, erudite, charming, nonsensical, and all the rest of the dribble we had sometimes spent a few hours drooling over. I did so want to talk to you, but you were stewed and I was busy working. Don't worry about the dough. Forget it. It doesn't bother me in the least, except that I hope it was enough to see you back to that drear spot in Canada.

I do hope, son, that you don't go overseas. I know you are depressed and can readily understand why, but, chum, don't, for Christ's sake, do anything as dumb as that. Stick it out for a while longer. Perhaps you can waggle a little more time later. If you know that you can get a few weeks, let me know a little beforehand, and I promise I will go out as your agent and hunt you a job myself.

So long, chum, and drop me a swift line.

ERROL

As a footnote to the above, it was five years before I was able to repay Flynn the one hundred and sixty clams. I was so happy to get back on the West Coast—as a civilian—I went down to the beach and dug the clams myself. I put 'em on ice and delivered them, together with my check, to Flynn.

Flynn's passing and the subsequent attacks on his way of life started me thinking. Didn't someone once say something about "he who casts the first stone"? Then there was another saying about how one should tidy up one's house first. Who are we to judge our fellow man? Was Flynn right or wrong in his way of life?

Here in sunny California, there's a saying to the effect that it is the cloud that makes one miss the sunshine. I didn't see Flynn very much during the last few years of his life. I missed him tremendously. I still do.

Index